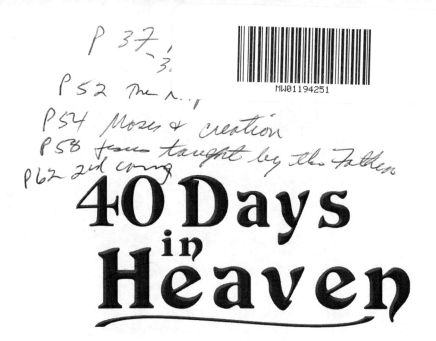

40 Days in Heaven

The True Testimony of Seneca Sodi's
Visitation to Paradise, the Holy City
and the Glory of God's Throne

– CENTENARY EDITION –

As transcribed by Rev. Elwood Scott
Edited by Edward Johnson

Editorial note:

The manuscript we received has been edited to relocate the author's interjections and original chapter divisions, which artificially divided the book according to Mr. Sodi's visits as he dictated his testimony to Rev. Scott, and which tended to interrupt the flow of the testimony itself. These parts have been preserved in the *End Notes* section.

We feel this is an improvement on the presentation of the testimony and helps the reader to stay absorbed in the beauty and transcendence of the heavenly domain without being distracted by what largely amounts to editorial comments. The original version can hopefully still be accessed by readers on the internet at www.spiritlessons.com, which is where we first discovered it in case one wanted to compare our treatment of it.

'First Fruits Offering' printing, 2008
This is the Second Edition, 2010

For on line publication
ISBN 978-145-05125-1-0

Published by King Edward Ltd
www.kingedwardltd.com

Bulk orders or custom print runs are available.
Please email books@kingedwardltd.com for enquiries.

P 13 angel explaining do him

CONTENTS

FOREWORD
Centenary Edition

The parting words from the Lord to Seneca Sodi were, "... so now I send you to make known what you have seen and heard, which is but a little of what you shall yet see, but this is all they will receive at your hand now...." And so He sent Seneca back to earth with a testimony of his 40-day visit to the Heavenly City which is the reward for the faithful.

The most memorable events in this testimony undoubtedly begin with Seneca's reunion with his close relatives in heaven, including his wife, mother, grandfather and his daughter. When he meets his grandfather, who died at an old age, he quickly sees that in heaven his vitality and youthful vigor have been fully restored. But an even greater surprise awaits him as he meets his daughter, who died while still in infancy—because she has since grown up into adulthood. She explained to him that children who have died in infancy before accountability are spared from ever experiencing pain or sorrow, but are raised to maturity by the angels, saints—even family members who have died and are now in heaven as well.

The second lasting impression is utter peace and security: the heavenly economy where everything is jointly owned and no one lacks any good thing; the heavenly atmosphere free from strife, sickness, fear and death; the heavenly calendar of timeless eternity with ample time to pursue every noble endeavor without hurry.

A third great assurance is belonging to the heavenly society of mankind, united into one large extended family where death bed conversions, innocent children from every nation who died of war, sickness or other tragedy, and saints of renown are all equally welcomed with the same acceptance and love as joint heirs with Christ of the whole of the heavenly kingdom. Seneca meets many martyred saints who have been rewarded for their struggles, and in fact joins a kind of picnic feast with a group of those who gave their lives for the testimony of the Lord.

For some the highlight may be Seneca's chance to discuss theology with Abraham, Moses, Isaiah, Paul and many others— for others still it could be the overwhelmingly glorious visit to the Throne of God. But whichever part is your personal favorite, I believe this testimony will strengthen the faithful, and impart the joy of being invited to spend eternity living in a city not made by man.

We find several common themes that are repeated throughout the narrative of this story, which are meant to leave a lasting impression on readers, including:

• That living for carnal purposes or in man's ways builds the substance of one's life with wood, hay and stubble, and none of this will pass into the heavenly hereafter but will be consumed and be lost. No heavenly reward is based on any such 'carnal' thing.

• People who haven't grown in true grace are unprepared for the greater things of God and so must spend time among the trees of life in paradise, partaking of the leaves of the trees which are for the healing of the nations, meaning for those who are unsanctified and only able to enter the 'outer courts' until they grow more in grace.

• That children who die are safe in heaven, and are raised in the most loving care imaginable by angels, saints and even relatives who have gone on to heaven before them, and who soon grow to maturity under their watchful care.

• The coming rapture and millennial reign of Christ are topics that are frequently talked about.

• That if people's hearts are not open to hearing the Truth from 'Moses and the Prophets,' meaning the Scriptures presented to them in an ordinary way, they are also not likely to be convinced of Truth should one testify who has returned from the dead. Not that people will not return from the dead and testify, since this fact has already been faithfully recorded in the Bible (Matthew 27:52), but merely that the weight of such a testimony will not convince those who are die-hard skeptics.

• Other more minor themes include the upward pull of saved souls toward God's Throne; that the rewards of heaven FAR outweigh the toils, sufferings and sacrifices of saints on the earth; that the heavenly glory is so wonderful that the thought of returning to the earth is dismissed by one and all; that in heaven everyone is quite active, mostly serving for the common good; and that those who suffered more on earth are now able to enjoy and praise the Lord more in heaven; and many more.

It is also interesting to note that it's been more than 100 years since this testimony first came to light, and far from proving to be an isolated story, such heavenly experiences are becoming more and more common. Some more recent testimonies which do much to substantiate this one include H. A. Baker's *Visions Beyond the Veil,* Mary K. Baxter's visitations to both Heaven as well as Hell.

Another testimony is from Rev. Oden Hetrick, who visited heaven at length, more than 80 times, and has many deep insights that again support much of this story by Seneca Sodi.

I also want to mention Anna Rountree who has written of her heavenly experiences in a series of books, *The Heavens Opened,* and *The Priestly Bride,* which confirm so many surprising elements and unique revelations of this story. Although her experiences are in a very different context, her books offer many details that match Seneca's testimony that could not be mere coincidence.

And there are numerous other accounts from old and young alike who have visited the eternal hereafter and been able to share indelible revelations of our true heavenly home—the place where we have eternal citizenship through faith in Jesus Messiah, the one we call Christ.

It is not that I am looking for support or confirmation to prove or defend the reliability of this testimony, since I think that is unnecessary. Besides Seneca's testimony predates these others in some cases by nearly 100 years, so the need for proof runs in rather the opposite direction.

I firmly believe this testimony can be trusted. We found it on-line and the Lord asked me to edit and re-print it, so I have it on His recommendation; and I hope you not only enjoy it, but also get to share it with your family and friends.

Nevertheless, there are some things to keep in mind when

reading any personal testimony of the spiritual world; the first of which is that Heaven is a very large place, The Holy City itself is 1,500 miles squared—cubed actually—so two people visiting, even for many hours each, may have vastly different experiences of the same general location, especially if they visit different parts of the City, or parts of the even more vast paradise outside the City walls.

We also find that people are able to perceive spiritual things slightly differently according to their own preparedness or spiritual maturity, something discussed in many of these testimonies.

So we see that personal testimonies of such a vast, complex, and highly spiritual place as Heaven need to be treated with some mature discretion. If the writers of the four gospel accounts all differed slightly in how they perceived and experienced the ministry of Jesus on earth, it is no wonder that others who visit heaven in a spiritual encounter have some slight differences in what they perceive and recollect as well. But as with the gospel accounts, the differences in many of these unrelated testimonies are far outnumbered by the bold similarities, sometimes in exacting detail.

Reading such testimonies is a great encouragement and does help to prepare us for what we have never even dreamed could be true. Yet even this body of writings and testimonies is not the key issue. Growing in love and grace is. So the main aim of this book is to offer a taste of the goodness of God, an unveiling of many mysteries, and a blessed assurance that our labors in Christ are not in vain, to encourage you to set aside all hindrances and press on to lay hold of the reward of the upward calling of God in Christ Jesus.

So with these things in mind, may you enjoy this spiritual classic that I believe will strengthen your faith and give you hope to endure whatever obstacles you encounter on your own journey on towards Paradise, the Holy City and the glory of the Throne.

We are blessed by the Lord to have received this testimony, and we pray that it in turn blesses you in these end days before most inspiring events overtake us all.

—Edward Johnson, Hong Kong
'First Fruits Offering' printing, 2008
Second Edition, 2010

INTRODUCTION
Rev. Elwood Scott, 1909

For many months past I have had frequent visits from a very peculiar visitor. Although his visits have been surprises to me, yet they have been most welcome indeed.

At first I was startled and greatly surprised when a man with silken beard and flowing garments came into my study entirely uninvited and without apology.

At first his visits were brief, then longer. If I went for an evening's walk in the fields or woods, he would frequently drop into my company, and seemed delighted to walk with me. I soon found he could speak different languages with perfect ease and that his nationality was different from my own.

He seemed of superior ability and his intellectual powers were far beyond my own abilities. In short, he was a very uncommon person.

I have had a custom for many years past of rising early in the morning and taking a drive for an hour or two before breakfast. Not infrequently I have overtaken a man who asked me for a ride, but on a number of occasions after I had welcomed the journeyman to my side, I found, Philip-like, by the side of the man in the chariot—that he was my silken bearded friend.

Frequently after an hour's conversation he would simply vanish from my presence without a moment's notice, and I have often looked in all directions, but was unable to see how he left.

I have been enthralled and lost in wonder and admiration at what he talks about, and the nature of his revelations. My soul loved him exceedingly and was grieved at his departure. Sometimes, after the family had retired, while busy at my studies he would suddenly come into my room and remain until after midnight.

Among his earlier visits, one evening he asked me if I could still write shorthand.

"Indeed," I said, "with as much ease as in earlier days."

"I have been looking for you for some time," he replied, "and if you consent to serve the purpose for which I have sought you, I will give a favored saint's blessing to you."

I gave him all the assurance I could that I would help him with any reasonable request he might make. He then lovingly replied:

"You shall then write a message for me to the people."

After the arrangements were all completed for its final settlement, he appointed an evening for a visit similar to those we had enjoyed so much when he took me by surprise. So from time to time we met and the results were the following pages which will explain this introduction. I am glad I consented to write for him. It has been with continual wonder, surprise, and admiration, and has also been a great blessing to me personally.

During one of his earlier visits he explained that he was the same man I had met some years before on the mountain slopes of the Cascades. I remembered him quite well, for I had spent a day and a night in his cheerful home, and under his holy influence. His name was Seneca Sodi, a Greek of Jewish descent, a fine scholar, a firm believer in Christianity, and a thorough student of his Bible.

But he seemed so changed now, and his face glowed with such a halo of light that I did not recognize him at first and was inclined to doubt his story and to let it all pass as a clever trick, that I could not explain, that was being played on me. Yet I could see a great similarity in appearance of this man and my long-bearded friend of the Cascades.

I said to him, "How can this be?"

He quickly replied, in the twinkling of an eye, "Only an earlier sheaf in the great resurrection harvest."

"Oh, my God!" I said, "Is it true that there is a man who has already experienced the great resurrection of the just, which is to occur at the last day?"

I thought then of the translation of Enoch, and of the chariot which swept Elijah into the heavens, of Moses, who twice fasted forty days and was alone with God upon the Mount of Vision until he had caught some of the radiance of the eternal glory. I thought of Paul who had been caught up into the third heaven and heard words of the everlasting kingdom. I thought again of the many bodies of the saints which slept and arose after our Lord's resurrection, who went about Jerusalem showing themselves alive from the dead. (Matthew 27:50-53)

So I reasoned within myself, saying, 'May not great events occur in these last days of Gentile grace? Why should not Seneca Sodi, one of the descendants of the ancient Israel of God, in these last days receive great revelations from the Almighty and an earlier resurrection than the rest of the great harvest?'

But I must leave him to tell his own story.

—Elwood Scott

CHAPTER ONE
Seneca Sodi's First Visit

It was the first day of June and the sun had set. The toil of the day was over. I had my studio thoroughly lighted and in the cleanest and best condition I could make It. I had provided pencils, paper, pens and ink, and was nervously waiting for my silken bearded friend. I felt a keen sense of uneasiness, not knowing the full nature of his mission or what all it might entail. I knelt and most solemnly prayed that the Almighty Father might be my helper, for my visitor had impressed me with a sense of awe, and I was quite humbled in his presence. The door at last opened and Seneca Sodi came in, a wonderful halo of light about his head and face.

I arose to greet him and with a pleasant "Good evening," he seemingly to grip my hand.

"My son," he said, "I greet you in the name of the Father." When he had taken a seat, he said, "Do you remember my humble home at the foothills of the Cascades?"

"Indeed I do, and the long walk among the hills we enjoyed together that day, and of the sleepless hours until after midnight, and of my promise to endeavor to see you again in your little earthly mansion of bliss."

"I could not wait for your return," said Seneca. "Strange experiences were awaiting me. I had been earnestly hoping that the coming of the Lord was near at hand and was much in prayer. I had the strange impression that great events were soon to come, but was not expecting the great favors which were so soon to be shown to me. But I find that God takes delight in surprising us with new and great blessings."

The Story Begins

Dinner had just been eaten and I had lain down on the couch for a few moments' rest. My two servants, Sena and Serva, were busy about the house, when all of a sudden, a blast of a trumpet called us all to the door.

A beautiful chariot of gold and two drivers clothed in white garments were standing very near. Immediately I seemed to fall into a trance and was lost to earthly things for a time. The angels came into the room and urged me to prepare quickly, saying, "For the Lord of the kingdom has need of you."

I could easily understand their errand and language. I was filled with triumphal praise in the thought of immediately going home. Resuming consciousness of earthly things, I quickly arranged with Sena and Serva, who had only seen glimpses of glory in flashes of bright light, but felt the presence of invisible ones about the room, to carefully guard my body, should I leave it behind. I found myself in a semi-conscious state, and saw a number of holy beings about my bed, for I felt so weary, I had lain down. I had momentary thoughts run through my mind, 'Is this really death? Am I really going to say good-bye to worldly things this day? Am I truly in the borderland of eternity? If so, blessed victory!'

I felt, now creeping into my soul, the raptures of eternal joy— oh, such light and visions of glory which were granted to me then! Spiritual truths and realities began to become very vivid to me, very clear to my understanding. I seemed to be passing into a large place where a new order of things existed. With one last effort to see and speak to my servants, I barely could say, "Good-bye," as I saw their anxious eyes looking into mine.

I heard some broken sentences and tried to explain, when I thought they were far out of hearing, and I closed my eyes only to open them in an eternal day.

The next thing I noticed was that I was standing in one corner of the room looking with deep interest upon my body, which was quietly lying dead upon the bed. I cannot very well describe the strange yet joyful feelings of my soul on finding myself released from the body. I came forward and stood beside the bed and with feelings of joy mingled with pity. I said to my body, "I feel sorry to leave you behind, but you are still mortal and will be till the resurrection."

I next saw three angels with me who seemed busy with some peculiar embalming process for my body, which I did not understand. They spoke to me most pleasantly and said, "Don't be afraid. We have come as your escorts to your heavenly home, the light of which shines so brightly upon you now."

How quickly I thought of that scripture: "The angels are all ministering spirits sent forth to minister for them who shall be heirs of salvation!" (Hebrews 1:14) I soon came to realize that physical eyes cannot see spiritual beings nor comprehend their movements except by some miraculous intervention, but that spirits can comprehend both matter and spirit.

I found that my vision was greatly improved since being freed from the mortal body—nor did I regret now that I was released, for everything seemed to shine with a luster and glow, with a brightness I had never known before, and what seemed more remarkable still, was that the sunlight did not help me in any way to see the things about me, for I knew it was night when all the world were asleep and that it was entirely dark to outward human eyes, yet to me everything shone with a splendor more grand than the brightest noonday earth ever afforded.

Again and again the scripture came to me: "Yea the darkness hides not from you, but the night shines as the day. The darkness and the light are both alike unto you," (Psalm 139:12) and again, "There shall be no night there." (Revelation 21:25)

I saw distinctly a number of angels about the room, each of which was covered with robes of pure and heavenly light, which made my soul so glad. I wondered why I could not have discerned them before, even while in the body. The scripture came to me where the prophet said: "The angel of the Lord encamps round about them that fear him and delivers them." (Psalm 34:7)

From this time I began to feel a strange upward leaping tendency. My spirit felt a mighty pull heavenward as though elastic cords were fastened to all parts of my soul, with the other end reaching into the skies.

Sena and Serva sat weeping by the bedside. I tried to speak to them, but could not get their attention. I walked near to them and laid my hand upon their heads, but still they did not comprehend me. They only seemed to weep more bitterly for there seemed to be a soul touch. Then again their tears would dry and they would scan the room as though some voice had been heard, and I felt sure they realized something of my presence without comprehending the truth of what was happening.

The angels now began to sing and oh such sweet music I never heard while in the body. When they had finished the song, they said, "Will you now follow us?"

When we had stepped outside, I saw the chariot which seemed to be made of light. It was standing still at the threshold. I understood its meaning and the special errand of the angels, and I wanted to jump in so strongly, as I practically shouted, "Hallelujah," which I am sure the angels heard, for they quickly said, "Glory to God in the highest."

I tried to say good-bye to my sleeping body, the old home and my two servants when the angels hurried me to a seat with them in the chariot. They again assured me of a safe journey homeward. In a moment more the chariot began to rise with a swift and noiseless motion, and, at what speed I could not tell, we were going on our flight toward the eternal mansions.

No sooner had I taken my seat in the chariot than I found I could converse with the angels with perfect freedom. There seemed to be a kind of comprehension of ideas without the effort of words, and yet we spoke as spirits speak. I have often heard words spoken while in the body which were wholly in the ear of the soul, and yet most distinctly understood when there was no audible voice whatever—the same as at St. Paul's conversion: he heard a voice distinctly in his inner consciousness while those who journeyed with him saw no man from whom the voice came.

I now asked, "Are you really and truly angels of God, about whom we have read and sung and heard so much while in the world?"

"Truly we are," they replied, "but of our birth you know nothing, for in fact we were not born but created, not in the earth but in celestial regions. We have learned our lessons in the past eternities in the presence of God, but we are glad to be your servants and helpers now, and this has been our glad service ever since man was created upon the earth, but we can tell you more about ourselves at another time."

I replied, "We have been strangers until this time, but you make me feel great confidence in your ability to safely guide the chariot. I have been looking forward to this time for many years, but did not know it was so near."

"Oh," said the charioteer, "you don't need to be afraid. I will bring you safely to your eternal home."

I looked out of the chariot again and saw we were moving with indescribable speed. The earth with its cities, towns and mountains was vanishing like a specter in the distance. We soon seemed to have the moon under our feet as we climbed the pillars of the heavens. We had much conversation on the way. I found the angels most tender and lovely beings, so full of instruction and helpfulness; my soul loved them exceedingly. I felt as though I was already acquainted with the heavenly kingdom, for the angels had told me so much. As I would look out from the chariot window, the stars could be seen everywhere just as I had always seen them from the earth; I knew then we had not gone beyond the regions of the solar system, so I asked the angel, "Where is heaven?"

"Oh," said he, "it is not far away. The earth is the first habitation of man, and while he is of the earth he is earthly in his nature. Heaven is the future and everlasting habitation of all those who have prepared themselves for it. You will soon find that my words are true that heaven is not far away. Your Father's love and care have provided both these worlds for you. Your heavenly home is your real home. The earth was only your birthplace, the place of your beginning. But when God gave you eternal life He connected you with all heavenly realms, for He gave you His life which has always been. Look and see," said he, for I was deeply thinking about these things for they meant so much to me now.

I looked around; we were just entering a region of bright clouds something like a glorious, glowing, earthly sunset, only far better. The time had been very brief indeed, but we were actually slowing down in the great suburbs of the eternal kingdom.

"Listen a moment," I said to the angel. "What music do I hear? Is it real or am I imagining it?"

"It is the song of the redeemed in heaven you hear. All the heavenly kingdom is full of music without a discord."

No sweeter music ever fell on my ears. I was perfectly enraptured with delight.

"Are we near the gates of the city?"

"Very near to the portals of paradise," he said. At this the angels bowed their heads and covered their faces with their hands, while I fell flat on my face in the chariot. Stillness reigned in our souls, but deep emotions began to heave in my heart. I felt I must break the silence by shouting the praises of God. The angels now began to sing with a sweet voice, "Holy, holy, Lord God Almighty! Just and true are all your ways, you King of Saints."

I sprang to my feet and for a moment seemed perfectly bewildered with what met my gaze in every direction. The light was so transparent and far exceeding the most perfect day earth ever afforded. Clusters of heavenly flowers were growing everywhere. Groves of beautiful trees loaded with fruit, along with magnificent flowering shrubs beautiful beyond description met my eye in all directions. Roadways like winding streets arranged with exquisite taste and beauty, were penetrating this pleasure ground of glory. Lovely souls were coming and going, passing and re-passing each other with the salutations and courtesies that heaven only knows.

The chariot was now slowing its speed and such raptures of glory which filled my soul, I cannot describe them! I was simply lost in wonder, while I kept saying, "Surely I am at home at last." The chariot seemed trembling as a thing of life and finally stopped beside a beautiful grove of fruit laden trees. The doors were opened and the angels stepped out. I practically sprang with one leap to the solid foundations of the heavenly kingdom. For a moment I stood perfectly entranced as I saw so many happy souls clothed in white garments of lovely patterns, and all with such bright and happy faces beaming with perfect contentment and satisfaction.

I could contain my feelings no longer. I fell on my face again beside the angel, with loud thanksgiving to God, and was in the act of worshipping the angel for his great care of and kindness toward me, when he said, "Worship God only! I am also a fellow servant of His, and this is my joyous service." At that he motioned to someone nearby. He came and was introduced as one of the elders of heaven, who gave me such a cordial welcome that my soul loved him intensely at once.

The angel now said, "I leave you in his care, but may see you again shortly."

I put out my hand toward him saying, "I am sorry to see you go; you have been such a friend to me. What can I do for your great kindness to me?"

"Oh, you can soon help others," said the angel. So waving with his hand, and with a lovely smile, he said, "Good-bye," and his chariot was gone.

The elder now said, "Well, my son, you are now at home. All that you see and infinitely more is the provision of your heavenly Father's love and almighty power. This is the borderland, my son, of the heavenly domain. Your sacrifices on earth were little when compared to your great gains here."

"Oh yes, and they were really nothing," I said. There comes to my memory a sweet passage of scripture which I never fully comprehended until now: "For our light affliction, which is but for a moment works out for us a far more exceeding and eternal weight of glory." (2 Corinthians 4:17)

"Sure enough," said the elder. "You have only begun to comprehend the glory; the weight of it you will yet feel."

"The grandeur and beauty of everything excels my highest expectation. Everything seems so real. Do tell me if I am imagining this, am I in a dream, or is it really true that I am in heaven?"

"Oh," the elder replied, "it is a common thing for souls when they reach the heavenly world to seem bewildered when first ushered into the presence of angels and the spirits of just men made perfect, and the glory of this kingdom. It does, indeed, exceed the most optimistic expectation. No, my son, you are not in a vision, you are really here. Your body indeed is left behind you, and you will find that you have many things to learn before you reach the Throne in the holy city. But be content, for I see you have thoroughly washed your robes and made them white before you left your earthly habitation.

"Be perfectly free," said the elder, "in asking any questions you may like, for the knowledge of this world is acquired by investigation and inquiry as was our earthly knowledge. Every desire you have will be fully met. All your cravings, desires and longings after the knowledge of your everlasting habitation have been fully provided for here. Your heavenly Father's will will be your will and all that you see, and infinitely more, are yours to enjoy forever. If you have made good use of your opportunities in your past life you have much treasure laid up in the city of which our Lord spoke while on earth and of which you will know more later on.

"I see," said the elder, "that over there is another soul just brought from earth to paradise whom I must go and welcome."

So saying, he went toward the chariot and there stepped out a lovely looking man, indeed, clothed in a robe of the purest white. The elder motioned me to him. As I came near and heard this conversation I found he was from the opposite side of the earth from which I had come. He spoke a different language from my own and yet I understood him well. In a moment he lifted up his hands and clasping them together he said, "Oh, bless God forever," at which we both fell on our faces with adoring praise to our Almighty Father. We continued a long time for our souls were overcome with the raptures of this place.

When we arose, another saint, apparently of ancient times, came to him, and said, "Let me assist you in the ways of the kingdom." I heard him ask him his name.

He answered, "I am Bohemond of northern Russia. Only a few hours ago I kissed my wife and children good-bye and embarked on a vessel on the White Sea at Onega bound for the North Cape. I only remember that the vessel was sinking and we were many fathoms below the surface. Oh, do tell me, is this heaven or is it but the mariner's dream of home, when he is far away?"

"My son," said this venerable father, "you have safely landed, not at the North Cape nor on the bottom of the White Sea, but in your eternal home. Your body no doubt is in the depths of the briny deep, but the angel was with you as the vessel went down and has brought you safely here. Your body will be cared for in the resurrection day of rewards."

The elder who was with me said, "How quickly we are gathering from all lands into our Father's house. This is only one of the many stations located in these distant portions of paradise. To these stations all souls come for their introduction into this heavenly home."

"How is that, will you explain to me?"

"Surely," he replied, "you will more fully understand as we go forward. You could not have endured the glory of the Throne without being prepared for it. Even now you could not endure the light so abundant within the city."

Just at this moment I saw a woman step from a chariot. She seemed to be so bewildered that she sank down as one of the attendants approached her. She threw up her hands and cried out in amazement, "Oh, my God! I am not worthy nor fit for this glory. Oh, can I ever be made right with God?" She closed her eyes almost unconscious with bewilderment and it seemed that she could not speak as her attendant kindly addressed her with most loving words. At last she opened her eyes and looked about in wonder and amazement exclaiming, "Oh, these white garments, these golden goblets, trees of life and blooming flowers! I am not worthy of them. Have I really a right to be here and to all these beautiful trees loaded with such lovely fruit? Oh, the mercy of God! I was such a great sinner."

"Yes, indeed," replied her guide, "but your sins have all been forgiven. The angels make no mistakes. You have a right to these

17

trees, for they are His on whom you have believed; yea they are yours, for you are His."

At this she arose to her feet and said, "But have I the wedding garment on? I was earnestly crying when the chariot came for me. I was in such deep distress and confusion of soul, knowing I had not been prepared for so great a change."

"You have been saved, my child," said her attendant. "So as by fire; you were not a faithful servant of God; you did not build with gold, silver and precious stones, but with wood, hay and stubble, which have been burnt. God cannot reward you largely now. These infinite blessings spread out before you in all directions may be obtained by and by, when you are prepared for them. Be faithful to your present opportunities, for much is before you to be done. Advancements which ought to have been made in the world will have to be made here before you can go on to the city gates, or see the shining glory of the jasper wall. Come with me and I will assist you in a further knowledge of Christ and His eternal salvation and kingdom."

I now said to the elder by my side, "Will you explain to me her great mistake?"

"Surely," he replied. "She represents a very large class in the world who have not made good use of earthly opportunities. She was never deeply interested in salvation till near the time of her death. Do you not see how gaunt and skinny she looks, and how little clothing she has, only a gown! Her repentance has been genuine and her faith accepted the promises of eternal life in her Lord, and her forgiveness has been complete. She has added but little grace and almost no growth to her soul. She now feels her great loss, as all such souls do and must feel. She has no treasure laid up in heaven. Paradise itself seems too good for her, but God in His great mercy will bring her on. These trees are for her. Their leaves are full of healing virtue. No one who has not received the gift of eternal life and been born again will ever be carried by the angels to this glory. Many, alas, perish from the earth in sight of the Redeemer's outstretched arms of love and mercy because they will not accept His gracious help; they love the pleasures of sin more than God or these everlasting joys and pleasures at His right hand here forevermore."

"Oh, blessed Christ," I said loudly, "filled with everlasting love and mercy for your people, that even in the last moments of life, like the dying thief, they may be snatched from the jaws of death! But, oh, her great loss, how sad!"

A group of happy souls now came toward us. The elder introduced us. We were soon acquainted and conversed with each other with great freedom, although we had never met before. We seemed perfectly acquainted in a few moments and the visit was very pleasant indeed. One man practically shouted the praises of God with loud hallelujahs, saying, "Oh, my God, I bless you. I am in heaven at last!" [a][1]

* * *

It seemed most wonderful to me upon finding that I could converse with perfect ease and freedom with anyone I met, although we had been accustomed to different languages and tongues while on earth, and often had to speak through interpreters, but now I found, since I had laid aside the material for the spiritual, I could easily understand the thoughts of anyone. As quickly as he could think I could read his thoughts. Matters of detailed explanation were not needed or required as I had been accustomed to while in the flesh, for if a subject was plain to any one with whom I was conversing, it seemed that at once it was just as clear to my own mind. So I was quite surprised to find how quickly I could take in a knowledge of the spiritual realm, and yet a second surprise constantly met me: that of the great depth of divine truth.

For instance, many things I had learned from the Holy Scriptures, while in my flesh, were now opened with a depth of meaning I had never seen before. I could compare it to nothing better than to great layer after layer and strata upon strata of precious mineral rock, so that the deeper down and the further on one went, the more precious became the ore and the finer the metal. I said to the elder by my side, "How is this?"

---

1. Superscript letters indicate an editorial digression removed to the *End Notes* section to improve readability.

He quickly and smilingly replied, "God never gives the best He has to give; you will find later on, that truth is unfathomable." I now felt myself like a little fish just launching out from the mouth of a great river into a great and boundless ocean without a shore to be seen or depth that could be sounded.

My feelings were joyful beyond any power to describe to a mortal man of flesh and blood. It seemed that my entire spirit was in a perfect rapture of delight. I asked the elder, who seemed to take delight in remaining with me, how I was to account for this rapturous joy which was increasing so constantly in my soul, until I felt I would break out into shouting and hallelujahs. He said, "The Spirit of God is the atmosphere of heaven; His joy becomes ours on a larger scale than we ever knew while in our flesh. The great joy that you feel now is only a little foretaste of what you will feel when you are ushered into the city and about the Throne."

Upon this I quickly remembered the Scripture where the prophet said: "In your presence is fullness of joy; at your right hand there are pleasures forevermore." (Psalm 16:11, Acts 2:28)

A feeling of praise was continually rising up in my soul causing me to want to speak it out. I wanted to praise God, for ever giving me an existence, and still more for my salvation from sin, for changing my heart and bringing me into this glory. Nothing of an earthly character could have induced me to have gone back to the world. I seemed to laugh at the thoughts of the fear of death, which fear belongs only to the unrepentant and the unsaved.

The elder, who seemed perfectly conscious of my desire, said to me, "You don't need to fear to give utterance to your feelings, for everyone praises God here. Those praise Him loudest and most who have learned how to praise Him best while on earth."

The elder, whom I found to be Joshua of olden time, and who had been taking such an interest in my introduction into the heavenly state, now said, "Let us go to that cluster of trees and sit down a moment." I noticed as we approached them that they were growing beside a great river whose waters were clear as crystal and sparkling with a light of which I had but a faint idea while I was in the flesh. The trees were beautiful beyond anything I had ever seen. Their form was so symmetrical and lovely, with no dead or withered branches. The leaves had such an aroma that the fragrance spread over everything and to all parts of the kingdom of God as I was told. Everyone was brought under its influence. I had felt the power of this fragrance long before I knew the source.

The elder now said to me, "Look across to the other side of the river;" where I saw clusters and groves of these trees lining the bank as far as the eye could reach. There I saw multitudes of redeemed souls clothed in the purest white and all of them seemed filled with the same spirit of praise which I had felt so constantly since entering the portals of the kingdom.

The elder again said to me, "Let us gather some of the fruit of these trees and then we will join that company over there."

I replied, "I would be quite glad to do so, for I have eaten nothing since leaving the body," and yet I felt no great sense of need. My hunger seemed more like what I had often realized while in the flesh when I felt a deep desire to hear a good gospel sermon.

My guide now said, "What kind of fruit would you prefer? You can have your choice of things here just as you used to in the earth. If you feel faint or weary from your long abstinence from food, this kind (pointing to a certain pear-shaped and beautifully colored fruit) is what you need, for the tree has twelve kinds, as you see, upon it."

I said with feelings of deepest praise, "Oh, how wonderfully God has provided for us! Twelve kinds of fruit on each tree, ripening their fruit every month, and the leaves never withering! Wonderful!"

"Here," said he, "pluck from the boughs on this side of the tree and eat." I did so, and much refreshing and enlightening grace as they imparted to me, it is beyond the comprehension of mortal man to know; it must be eaten to be understood. The taste of the fruit was delicious indeed. The earth never furnished anything like unto it for taste, not the orange, peach, nor melon. Nor would the fragrance of the rose compare with it. "When anyone eats of these trees," said the elder, "he can never die again, grow older nor feel weary; death has no more dominion over him. One of these trees grew in the Garden of Eden. After our first parents had sinned against God, they thought to eat of the fruit of it also, but God said, No, for had they eaten of it they would always have lived in that sinful, dying state. So a flaming angel was sent to guard it, and so man never eats of it until he has passed the boundaries of his earthly life."

"Now," said Joshua, "let us cross over." To my great astonishment I found we could walk upon the surface of the water, which seemed like a sea of glass, it was so transparent, and yet it was gliding and rolling along as beautifully as any stream I had ever seen on earth. I quickly remembered the Word of God by His prophet: "But there the glorious Lord will be unto us a place of broad rivers and streams; wherein shall go no galley with oars, neither shall gallant ship pass thereby." (Isaiah 33:21)

As we walked along, I asked him, "How is it that we do not sink in the water?"

He said, "You seem to have forgotten that you have left your body behind you, and that you are now ready to be clothed upon with a far more excellent body than you have ever known. Your spirit cannot sink in these waters. You will soon find that you can go from place to place at will either in the air or upon the solid foundations of the celestial country, but let us go quickly," he said, for I was inclined to linger at every fresh object I came in contact with, "for I must introduce you to that great company you see over there."

As we went on, I glanced up and down the river and saw many other spirits, still later arrivals than I, passing on toward the gathering legions of the blood-washed. Among them was my friend, Bohemond of Russia, whom I met as he stepped from the chariot only a short time before.

My soul was filled with such an inexpressible sense of praise to God for the unspeakable gift of eternal life and for such a rational sense that it was I, myself, who once had lived in a world of sorrow and death, the memory of which, with a conscious freedom from it, now filled my soul indeed with ecstasies of eternal joy. [b]

*   *   *

By this time we had climbed the eastern bank and were approaching near to a multitude of happy spirits. Many of them turned toward me. The elder now said, "You will feel yourself entirely at home with them." And after a brief word of introduction, he said, with a pleasant smile, "Good-bye, I will see you again," and he was gone. Among the very first I met was the spirit of a dear man, an old friend of mine in Norway, and one whom I had known from his childhood. I had said farewell to him at a foreign port nearly four years ago and had not heard a word from him since, till I saw him among this multitude. We were soon face to face. He looked bewildered and in wonder.

I said, "Truly, is this you, Mr. Hansen, the friend of my youth?"

"Oh, indeed, and is this the face of Seneca Sodi?" And with that we embraced each other in our arms as redeemed souls only can.

"I was not looking for you now," I said to him, "you looked so well and strong when I saw you last."

"Oh, yes, indeed, but I am here, and nothing could induce me to go back." He asked me, "How long since you came?" I was just proceeding to answer him when another stepped near to us whom I had known so well for many years. She was a noble Christian woman and a faithful servant of Christ in His vineyard on earth, who had turned many to the Lord. I had not heard of her departure from the earth, but here she was with such a halo of light about her head that at once I thought of the words of the Lord: "They that be wise shall shine as the brightness of the firmament, and they that turn many to righteousness as the stars forever and ever." (Daniel 12:3)

I saw also among the great company the spirit of an infant which had so recently passed away. The one taking care of it said its mother had wept and grieved much and many had tried to comfort her on the day of its death, but that her sorrow was too great to receive much consolation. 'Oh!' I thought. 'If she could only see it now in this glory and with such care she would quickly brush away her tears and rejoice in the way God has provided for all His children.' I at once began to think of many of my friends and dear relatives who had gone on many years before. Where are they now? I wondered. So I asked one of the earlier arrivals if he knew the system or order here, in reference to those who had left the world years ago. "Oh," said he, "they have gone on to the city itself, of which you see the light over there in the distance," pointing toward the source of the river.

"Shall we not go there soon ourselves?" I asked.

"Yes," said he, "as soon as our company is made up, which is now nearly full."

I looked across the river from whence I had just come, and saw quite a number gathering about the trees and could hear them most clearly shouting, "Bless the Lord, oh my soul!" I saw others gathering from various points all of whom seemed to have escorts or ministering spirits to guide them in their first introduction into the heavenly country.

I thought again of that precious word of God: "Carried by angels into Abraham's bosom." Abraham's joy is certainly come now, I whispered to myself. Then I modestly and reluctantly asked, "Is Abraham anywhere about here?" and referred to that Scripture just quoted.

"Oh!" they said, "he was just here just a little while before you came, but was suddenly called into the city on some important errand, for everyone here is engaged in a joyous service for our Lord. No doubt he will be here again soon as he or someone of the elders or ancients always guides these gathering multitudes to the gates of the city."

I seemed now to be conscious that we were somewhere near one of the great entrances or gateways into the heavenly world, where all the souls from certain sections of the earth are brought and welcomed. From the very moment of my departure from the body there was a constant and mighty drawing of my soul upward toward the Throne of God. It seemed scarcely possible for me to remain upon the earth even to take one last look at terrestrial things, for I knew I had passed beyond the limits of time into a boundless eternity; I wondered deeply why I felt that strange feeling and tendency to leap upward, and so I felt a freedom to ask one near me if he could give me an explanation. "Oh!" said he. "We all felt just the same. It is the law of spiritual gravitation which draws all beings, which have been purified and made holy, to this great kingdom where God is. No doubt you have often felt something of it while yet in the flesh. Sometimes you inwardly sighed and wished to be freed from your mortal flesh. The pull of this force was such that during sickness or severe trouble you have often said, 'Oh! That I had the wings of a dove, then would I fly away and be at rest.' (Psalm 55:6) It was that which made St. Paul say as you will no doubt remember: 'It were better for me to depart and be with Christ.'" (Philippians 1:23)

"Ah, yes," I replied, "I see that now, but it is not the case, I am sure, with all souls when they leave the body without any regard to their moral or spiritual state."

"Oh, no," said my friend, "there are two great centers in the spiritual universe of God. They might be compared to the two poles of a magnet, with which no doubt you were acquainted while in your probationary state, the positive and the negative. All souls are drawn toward one of these two places, according to their respective condition. God's Throne is the great center of his everlasting kingdom of light; toward it, all gracious spirits, who are blood-washed, are drawn from the time they accept Christ and were born of Him, with more or less conscious power according as they yielded themselves to his holy will, and were transformed into his blessed image."

"I understand fully what you mean," I replied. "I knew something of it while in my earthly life and have often spoken of it to those around me, but will you tell me, in a word, more about those who chose a sinful life in the world?"

"Just the opposite," he replied. "They are drawn with a mighty force downward toward the pit of eternal death, where death shall always reign."

Just at this moment I saw one coming toward me whom I recognized as my old grandfather, who had been gone from the earth for more than thirty years. He was a very faithful servant of God during his lifetime on earth. He was old and gray when he left us, but here he was in the beauty and vigor of manhood. "Oh, Seneca!" he said. "You are home at last."

"Indeed," I said, as I embraced him in my arms, embracing each other with a love-kiss earth never knew. His words of welcome were so heavenly. We both shouted out, "Bless the Lord, oh, my soul!" He asked many questions about relatives and friends, the condition of the church where he used to worship, how long since I left the earth, etc., but I soon found that his questions were more like the queries of one of the elders of heaven when he asked the beloved disciple in Patmos: "What are these that are arrayed in white robes? And whence came they?" (Revelation 7:13) The elder knew better than John himself. I soon discovered his superior knowledge even of terrestrial things which had transpired long since his day on the earth. I remembered then—oh how strongly!—that in the blessed Book it says that the angel which talked with John while in Patmos said: "I am your fellow servant, and of your brethren the prophets, and of them which keep the sayings of this book." (Revelation 22:9) I said to him, "How is it you know so much about the things of the world since you left it?"

"Oh!" said he. "We have great liberty here in the vast domain of this great kingdom of Almighty God. Many have come since I entered the portals of heaven whom you know well. We have had many long and precious visits. They have told me much."

"I trust that in due time we can have such a visit," I replied, "for I am so glad to have met you."

"Indeed we will," said grandfather, "but here comes Abraham and I want you to meet him."

"Sure, I shall be made happy beyond my power to tell you for I have read and heard of him all my life. Oh, my soul! So many wonderful favors are shown me."

CHAPTER TWO
Meeting Abraham

"Are you sure it was Abraham you saw?" I asked my grandfather.

"Oh, indeed! I know him well."

"Then," I replied, "I shall be quite glad to see him, for as you know, his name was a household word among us on earth. Will you please tell me which one he is, for there are so many saints in shining garments coming and going. I was asking about him just before I met you. I used to wonder very much what he looked like, and have often thought I would be delighted to see him. I have greatly admired his faith that never staggered, and his obedience to go where his eye could not see. How precious to us were the words concerning him: 'Abraham believed God and it was counted unto him for righteousness.' (Romans 4:3)

"I do not see him at present," said grandfather, "but he was among that group over there that is coming along the bank of the river. He has turned away from us just for a little while, for I see he has gone to welcome a company of new arrivals, who have just crossed the river. I see by his movements he intends to bring this company to the city, where they will be introduced to the Lord Himself."

"But grandfather, if we go on to the city right now will I see you again?"

"Oh, yes," said he, "I shall be there quite often and we shall have much opportunity to talk about all past events, as well as what is before you. I have many things I wish to say to you. After you have been recognized by our Lord Jesus and confessed before His Father and the angels, you will then have abundant liberty to go as you will. I have just come from the Throne itself and have left many that you will recognize when you are there. Your dear mother, who has been gone from you for more than fifty years, is aware that you have entered the portals of the heavenly kingdom. She would have come with me at this time for she is very eager to see you, but she was detained on some very important matters for her Lord. No doubt she will meet you before you arrive at the city gate, but just now I must hurry on for there is an old friend with whom I was a playmate in earth, who has just arrived. We were bound together like David and Jonathan. When I left the earthly shores, he took it very hard, and now for many years he has been very lonely. He has just been carried by the angels into this our glory and I am going now to give him my welcome and bring him to this great company. There is an unusual stir about the Throne today which Abraham can explain when you meet him. He will introduce himself when he comes. I hope to return in time to go with you up to the city," and waving his hand he said good-bye.

I watched my old grandfather as we used to call him in the earth. He walked off so gracefully or rather sprung like a young man. He used to be so old and decrepit, but now his youth is renewed like the eagles' and every expression of his face was joy.

At this moment I turned around and to my great joy a most lovely person was coming very near me. He bore marks of great age, and yet for all that, he had an indescribable youthful appearance. He was not like the other spirits that I was accustomed to seeing. The elder that I first met and he were very much alike.

"Is this Abraham?" I said.

"It is," he replied.

"In the bosom of Abraham!" (Luke 16:22) I said softly, and began to bow myself down before him, for a certain feeling of awe filled my soul.

"Stand up, my son," he said, "we are all brethren here." Then he took my hand in his and with his other drew me close to him and gave me his kiss of welcome. Oh, such a freshness of love and joy which burst upon my soul, so that I practically shouted, "Hallelujah," and said again, "In the bosom of Abraham!"

"Do you remember that Scripture?" he said. "Well, you will realize its meaning more and more, but who is this by your side?"

"Bohemond," I replied, "who also has just come from the world."

He then gave him his cordial welcome and said, "The great joy and gladness which you now feel has been mine during a hundred generations of earthly Lives. Someday I trust I can introduce you to Lazarus, of whom it was said by our Lord: 'He was carried by angels into Abraham's bosom.'

"I see," said he, "you have just arrived and have much wonder and many questions to ask about this heavenly kingdom of our Lord. While we talk for a few moments let us be refreshed with a drink from this crystal river, for it flows from the great palace up at the Throne. Would you like to taste its waters?"

"Oh, indeed we would, I have sung hymns, and read in the Holy Scriptures concerning this very river, where the angel pointed it out to John, who in his vision saw it proceeding out of the Throne of God and the Lamb." (Revelation 22:1)

He now proceeded to the brink and with a golden goblet he dipped and filled the cup for me, and another for Bohemond, and said, "My sons, drink of this river and you shall never thirst again, nor be faint, nor weary for its lack, for its waters shall never fail."

As I drank from the cup I said, "Oh praise God for such a supply! So sweet to the taste! How full of invigorating power! It makes me feel the joy and glow of youth."

"You never can feel old or weary again, after drinking of this living water," said Abraham, "for it is the Water of Life. I just now gave a drink to a company of fresh arrivals before coming to you. Did you not hear them praising God? They, with that great group near them, are now learning to sing together, the song in which you will join them, which we will all sing at the city gate

29

shortly. Some of them have it quite well now and others knew it when they came, for it is contained in the Holy Scriptures on earth. God has revealed the order so that all might be familiar with it. Do you remember the song?"

"Please repeat it for me," I said, "that I may know which song you mean."

He replied, "John was caught up in spirit so he heard the strains of this music and wrote: 'I heard a great voice of much people in heaven, saying, "Alleluia, salvation, and glory, and honor, and power unto the Lord our God." And God from the Throne said, "Praise our God all ye His servants, and ye that fear Him, both small and great." And I heard as it were the voice of a great multitude, and as the voice of many waters, and as the voice of mighty thunderings, saying, "Alleluia. Let us be glad and rejoice and give honor to Him, for the marriage of the Lamb is come, and His wife has made herself ready."'" (Revelation 19:1,5-7)

"Oh, yes," I replied, "I remember that song so well and can join with them singing it now." I said, "Father Abraham, shall we not soon go on to the Throne? I have such a desire to see my Lord Jesus, I have loved Him these years, and then I have many loved ones beside that I feel sure are about the Throne."

"Your desires, my son," he replied, "shall be fully met. The patience you have leaned on earth is of great service to you here. So I hope you will feel that restful, quiet trust in all God's ways."

"Oh yes, my whole soul says, 'Your will be done.'"

"You will soon see the King in His beauty, and probably some of those who knew you best may come out and meet us on the journey toward the city gates, for they certainly know you are here. Just as soon as our company is full we will be off. Twelve legions make the company, and you see they are gathering from all directions.

"Look down the stream and you can see another company quickly filling up. Look across to the other side and farther up the stream and you see another. The guides who welcome them soon know to what company and place each belong. Some have made but little preparation for this glory when they left the world, and now the light is too great for them, and, as you see, they fall back into the rear and are content among the trees, waiting to become more prepared by applying these wonderful leaves of the trees. But all these companies you see will soon be gathering about the gates of the city."

* * *

"Father Abraham, may we ask you a question while we are waiting for these gathering numbers that make this company?"

"Certainly," he replied, "use your greatest freedom."

"I have just met my old grandfather, who has been here for more than thirty years. I had a long talk with him before you came. He has told me many things concerning this eternal world of light, but just as he was leaving me, to welcome another friend of his, he said there was considerable commotion about the Throne just now. Would you care to explain it to us?"

"Oh, most gladly. Great events are about to occur of the most interesting character that time and eternity have ever known. Our Lord has recently announced that the time has nearly arrived when He shall leave the mediatorial throne and in company with all the saints and angels, will descend to the earth for its judgment, for the cup of its iniquity is now nearly full."

"Oh," I replied, "we have been expecting Christ's coming to the earth for many years. Some had even gone so far as to have dates set when He would return."

"But," said Abraham, "that was their folly. Our Lord had distinctly told them as you will remember in His word, and we have faithful copies of the Holy Scriptures here in heaven to which we have access whenever we choose, that no man knows the day nor the hour—even the angels themselves did not know nor even now do they know. (Matthew 24:36 , Mark 13:32) None of us who have been here during great cycles of eternity have known when the time would be and even now the exact period has not been announced. But notable events are announced at the Throne during the great convocation, when millions of saints and angels meet up for the great praise services of which you will know more later. All of us here, like those upon earth, are deeply interested in this great event, which the Father has kept in the secrets of His own counsels.

"The church on earth and in heaven will soon unite in one great jubilee and celebrate the final and great victories of the cross of our Lord, at the resurrection of all the saints, from the days of Abel to the end of the age. The living saints of earth as you know will all be changed in a moment, in the twinkling of an eye, and with divine permission and arrangement, we in heaven will all go back to the cradle of our nativity and say good morning to the church on earth. Then the great resurrection shall occur. Then will follow the earth's great Sabbath. Although we have been here for long ages, yet we have looked with great interest towards this event. Tender memories cluster about the scenes of childhood and early youth, and we feel glad to know we shall soon visit the place of our early experience in the world and the scenes that witnessed our salvation from sin. And then we shall receive the fullness and completion of our salvation, the redemption of our bodies. A very few of us have already had our resurrection as you see in my own case."

"I have been waiting for some time to ask," I replied, "what made the great difference between your appearance and those other happy spirits and even my own?"

"All the elders," said he, "received their resurrection at the time our Lord was raised and with Him became the first fruits of those who slept, yet we ourselves shall be freshly dressed up along with you for the marriage of the Lamb, a great event to which we all are looking."

"Oh," I said. "Blessed be the Lord our God! My soul is in perfect rapture for His unspeakable gift."

"You may well be," said Abraham, "and it will never die away from your soul. The time is almost here and the angels and saints have carried the news to the utmost limits of this heavenly domain. The Holy Spirit also, who is the light of the church on earth, as well as in heaven, is impressing the minds of the most godly in the church militant with this great event. I will speak to you again of this if you desire, but I see our company is now about full and we must prepare to be off for the holy city.

"The behavior, you will find, of all this great crowd will not be the same, although nearly all are fresh arrivals from the earth, and with few exceptions all are eager to see the King in His beauty. Some were exceedingly joyous, but others not so much so. Some have not made good use of their opportunities while on earth, and have not filled their souls with good. They have not been given to much prayer and efforts to develop the fruits of the spirit with themselves, which makes up our character for eternity. They have been building with wood, hay and stubble, instead of gold, silver and precious stones. But feel yourselves entirely at ease, for we shall soon be off for the city."

Again he passed us, and stopping, said, "I see what you are looking at. You have been noticing some who, as we have been preparing for our journey to the city and the Throne, are inclined to drop into the rear, and are not so much filled with rejoicing."

"Yes," I said, "and I think I understand it. I remember while on earth, many of God's children never could be persuaded to enter wholeheartedly into the way of life. Their faith was weak and unsatisfactory, and in times of great rejoicings in God, they had but little appetite for the deeper things of the kingdom. They lacked what we called real true consecration to God. Sometimes, we almost questioned whether they were saved from past sins. It was a rule among us that those who had a clear knowledge of much forgiveness always loved much, and those who were filled with the blessed Holy Spirit, had a sense of great victory over the world, the flesh and the devil, and were of those who overcame and had right to the tree of life and to enter in through the gates into the city. These were filled with great rejoicings of soul, and it seems that the same attitudes are extended into the heavenly kingdom."

"You are quite right, my son," said Abraham, "and when those, lean in soul, arrive here, they have but little desire for the crystal river, nor could they enjoy the fountains at the Throne, nor do they have great desire for the fruit upon the trees of which no doubt you have been eating. When they come here they mostly partake of the leaves, the fragrance of which is so sweet and powerful to you."

All the time he was speaking to me there was constantly coming to my mind the words of the apostle: "Every man's work shall be made manifest, for the day shall declare it because it shall be revealed by fire, and the fire shall try every man's work of what sort it is. If any man's work shall abide which he has built there upon, he shall receive a reward. If any man's work shall be burned, he shall suffer loss, but he himself shall be saved, yet so as by fire." (1 Corinthians 3:13-15)

"Oh," I said, "how blessed that they have the foundation itself, the atonement made by our Lord Jesus Christ, and the privilege of these leaves which I remember are for the healing of the nations." (Revelation 22:2)

Abraham then said to me, "God cannot reward them largely, for their lack of capacity to receive, and yet as full as they are prepared to do so they will enjoy the glories of this heavenly kingdom. One star differs from another star in glory. (1 Corinthians 15:41) They that be wise shall shine as the brightness of the firmament and they that turn many to righteousness as the stars forever and ever." (Daniel 12:3) [c]

* * *

By this time everything was ready and we were off. Twelve legions of souls from various places had gathered in a very short time beside the river and all had come by the way of the cross. It did not matter what language we had known on earth, we could fully understand each other there, and all were speaking, as we passed along, of the precious salvation through Jesus. As I turned myself from the themes of my former conversation and began to mingle more freely with the group of joyous spirits, I met some whom I recognized as old friends. One dear lady whom I had known as an invalid for many years, and yet a very spiritual Christian, was in the group. She was rejoicing with exceeding joy. I cannot tell how we recognized each other, but there is such a similarity of the spirit itself to the bodily features that we at once knew each other, and memory was so fresh that we seemed never to have forgotten anyone. She seemed so well now, and her face was beaming with immortal youth. As I drew near to her there was a halo of light and heavenly joy, beyond my power to describe to you, covering all her soul. As I spoke to her, calling her by name, she at once seized my hand, exclaiming, "Glory be to the Father. Saved, saved, forever! All sickness and suffering over! Hallelujah!"

"Yes," I said, "and how well you look. Old things are passed away."

"Indeed, when you knew me I was a great sufferer. I realize now Paul's words: 'For our light affliction which is but for a moment works for us a far more exceeding and eternal weight of glory.' (2 Corinthians 4:17) My soul is so full of glory. We are getting so near the King in His beauty. Oh, listen! What do I see and hear? Oh, the chariots of God are coming!"

At this we practically shouted, and could hear very lovely music in the distance, and looking in the direction from whence it came, we saw a great procession of angels with flaming chariots of light coming toward us. I cried out, together with many other voices, as we caught the first glimpse of them.

"Oh, Father Abraham, is this our Lord Jesus for whom we have been eagerly looking so long?"

Abraham lovingly replied, "These are the chariots of God under the control of angels. They will soon be among you, bringing many ancient loved ones to greet you with a welcome when they carry you to the city and the Throne itself. You remember how it was on earth, when our friends came from long journeys, how we would go long distances to meet them. I used to go far down from Hebron to welcome Lot and his children. Isaac went a long way into the fields when he knew the camels and Rebecca were coming. In your day you went to the railroad stations and the wharfs of the shores to meet your loved ones. They keep up this custom in heaven."

In a few moments more—swifter by far than the fastest express trains of earth—they came nearer and nearer, and with a great sweeping circle they seemed to pass us by, but at Abraham's suggestion the great legions now parted, standing in two long groups with an open space or aisle between, to give the chariots room to pass. Soon, they began to reduce their speed and moving slowly but most graciously they passed between the long rows of awestruck, expectant souls. We all stood as in breathless silence not only awestruck but in amazement and great wonder, at the marvelous sight. The chariots and all within glowed with a brightness and glory which we knew were reflected from the Throne itself. So when they had finally stopped, they gave one great shout of hallelujah to God, saying, "His redeemed are here!"

No sooner were the chariots standing among us than we saw that they were filled with happy, shining ones. They soon sprang out and were among us. They had come to meet and welcome us to these realms of everlasting light and day. But who were they but acquaintances, friends and relatives whom we had known so well on earth, and who knew of our coming. We used to have reunions on earth, but they could in no wise compare to the joy of this meeting. Some of these had been there for many years. In a few moments more, many were embraced in each other's arms. Oh, such joy I never knew before, and such welcome! "Oh, blessed rewards!" I shouted.

Among these was my own dear mother. She had died many years ago. How she knew me I cannot tell, nor how I knew her I do not know, but she rushed toward me and I knew her so well and said, "Oh, mother, is this you?" She was beautiful and lovely. She embraced me in her arms and said, "I knew you were coming." The memories of childhood and all her customary smiles and kindness which a mother's love suggests, came back to me. There were many others like myself. Mothers and sons, fathers and children, old friends meeting again. The glory and joy of the occasion excelled anything I had yet known. The charioteers now kindly invited us all to take passage with them. We of course accepted their offers of kindness with thankfulness and were soon inside the chariots and the whole multitude were praising God. In a few moments we were flying with great speed toward the city gate, following the course of the river.

"The light toward the city which I had seen on my first arrival, grew more and more glorious as we neared the city. We could at length see the shining of the jasper walls. Although we were rolling along at such great speed the wheels were noiseless and the chariots without a bump. The appearance of the landscape on either side seemed at a distance like a sea of glass mingled with fire, but on a closer examination it seemed that it was immortal. Flowers of unfading glory, and with an endless variety of colors, many of which I never saw anything before to which I could compare them and their indescribable loveliness attracted everyone's attention. We saw thousands of angels and happy spirits passing in all directions, but all I saw seemed very joyous and happy in their work. I thought of the word of the Lord: "He makes his angels spirits and His ministers a flaming fire." (Psalm 104:4, Hebrews 1:7)

I said to my mother, "Can you tell me why we were not brought directly to the Throne at once when we departed from our earthly home?"

"Oh," said she, "you could not have endured its glory, but would have been dazzled into utter confusion and unconsciousness. Even now your expanding powers cannot take in all the glory and grandeur of the city until you are further prepared for it. The same law prevails in heaven as on earth. The Patriarchal and Jewish systems were very inferior to the Christian dispensation and the kingdom of heaven on earth was very inferior to the kingdom here, as you see, in point of glory and blessing. So you could not be ushered in about the Throne till you were graciously prepared for it. But I am so glad you are here. I had word of your coming before you reached the portals of paradise, and I have often had word concerning you since I left you. This very angel which you do not recognize, who is your charioteer, has often been to you. Once when you were very ill and away from your home and came well near dying, he was by your bed all the night and laid his hand upon you and said you should live and finish your work. He has told me how he saved you on the water once when you came near being drowned."

"Oh, mother, was he there at that time?"

"Indeed, my son, and his own hand righted your little boat when it was almost overturned."

"Well, mother, I always felt there was some mysterious Providence which saved us that day, but how little I knew this angel of heaven was with me then. Oh, thank God for His wonderful care!"

"Yes," said mother, "at one time, he told me he kept you from getting on a railroad train, which if you had, your life would have been lost, and your work not been done. Do you not remember many times when strange Providence came into your pathway and you wondered and sometimes grieved at such occurrences? He was guarding your life and shielding you from the stormy blasts of danger. Some day you can ask him all about these times, and we ourselves will talk it all over, for we are just in the springtime of our eternal life. But do you see we are nearing the golden gate, glistening with one great pearl, studded with a thousand shining gems? In just a little while we will all join in singing the Song of Moses and the Lamb? Do you know it?"

"Yes," I replied, "for we have been singing it far back in paradise where this great legion was made up." I repeated it over in a subdued tone to my mother, but wanted to shout it out at the top of my voice.

"Here," said she, "take this harp I have brought for you." She loosened it from a golden belt about her and gave it to me. "See, I have one like it."

CHAPTER THREE
Just Outside the City Walls

ust as we were coming near the great gateway one of the elders came and met us, saying, "All welcome, ye children of God. Your Redeemer stands just inside the gate over there at which you will soon enter." The elder made such a lovely bow and his words were so cordial and full of love it seemed to send a thrill of gladness over every soul.

I looked up at the majestic wall. It was of great height and shone with a brightness I cannot describe. It rested on twelve massive foundations, each having the name of one of the apostles above it, and so they decreased to the twelfth and presented the appearance of a majestic stairway. The name of Peter was written on the first foundation, Paul on the second, John on the third, James on the fourth, and so on to the top. From this topmost foundation, garnished with an amethyst, the wall rose to a great height. The light streaming from these foundations was most precious. Just here I noticed Abraham passing nearby, and I asked him the mystery of the wall and its foundations.

"Oh," said he, "this wall is the eternal security of God's people. As long as this wall shall stand they are eternally safe. The mighty truths of God, promulgated by the apostles, as taught by our Lord Himself, is our eternal safety. Certain of the angels many long years before my time on milk, abode not in the truth, and God cast them out and they fell into eternal darkness and shame. But now this wall, of which you can see but a very little portion, entirely encircles this giant city, and within the truths suggested by these foundations we shall ever abide, going in and out and finding everlasting comfort. You see that great Judean gate over there? Its frame and hinges are of the purest gold and set with one great pearl. This gate always stands open for there is no restraint in heaven. Unbounded liberty is now yours forever. And the wall has respect to these outside as well as to those inside. The angel at the gateway is to give direction to all who may inquire. You will further remember that there are twelve of these gates as well as twelve foundations and there are twelve angels as well as twelve gates. No man can enter these gates not fully prepared. Did you notice some who dropped back far into the rear? In the world the truth had to be observed for any advancement. This wall with its gates marks a definite experience in the journey of the redeemed. It is a fuller development of the great truths suggested by the ancient tabernacle, the holy and the most holy place has reference to the saints on earth and those in heaven."

Just at this time I noticed many happy souls with the glory of God upon them, coming through the gateway toward us. They were all clothed in the purest white and each with a harp in his hand. As they drew near us, there began to be a general recognition of each other. These had been redeemed from the sections of the earth from which we had come. Many of them were old friends who had passed from the earth many years ago, yet whom we had known so well in early life and as soldiers in the Lord's army many of us had fought His battles together.

The recognition was so full and memories so fresh it seemed as only yesterday when we had parted from them, when they said good-bye and sailed toward the harbor. There was no attempt to restrain feelings for they could not be restrained. It was one 'hallelujah' to God. They seemed as much delighted as we. I thought again how weakly we had believed God's word in the earth and yet how divinely true it was. We spent a long time in shaking hands and in love's embrace, with a conscious sense that we were now united in an eternal union. I thought again of Paul's words: "Now we see through a glass darkly, but then face to face." (1 Corinthians 13:12) Many angels were mingling among us and seemed in great delight at witnessing our joy.

One of them said to me, "We have been watching over you since your infancy in the world, looking forward to this very time. We rejoice with you and have an increasing joy as we behold your own."

Abraham now stood up prominently before us all and with his hand motioned for silence, and said, "I wish now to repeat to you all a portion of God's Word which I know you will recognize: 'But ye are now come unto Mount Zion and unto the city of the living God, the heavenly Jerusalem, and to an innumerable company of angels, to the general assembly and church of the first born which are written in heaven, and to God the Judge of all, and to the spirits of just men made perfect and to Jesus the Mediator of the new covenant, and to the blood of sprinkling which speaks better things than the blood of Abel.'" (Hebrews 12:22-24)

Indeed it brought it fresh to all our memories, for our hearts were burning with great emotion, but scarcely did we know what to say, we were so over-awed at our surroundings, and the real consciousness that it was ourselves and our friends who had met in an undying state and in a sinless country, and in the presence of some who had lived thousands of years ago amid customs so different from our own, also face to face with the angels of whose beginning we knew nothing, among all whom I saw none who seemed aged or feeble. Some that I had known in the earth as old men now seemed young and the very picture of health and enjoyment. The angels also were clothed with youthful appearance and vigor. I said to one of them, "How is it that the passing of so many years does not make its mark upon you here?"

"Oh," said the angel, "one day here is as a thousand years of an earthly existence. No one ever grows older in appearance or feelings in this world. We are undying and undecaying. We are clothed only with immortality. No one ever feels a pain or knows a sorrow here."

Just at that moment, a woman who had been standing near and listening to the conversation, clapped her hands with ecstatic joy and said, "Oh, blessed be God for such a deliverance! I was greatly afflicted for thirty years before I was released from my earthly pain and sorrow. I was reduced to poverty and want, often spending many days and nights alone and lonely. My sickness was of long duration and my suffering was great. Occasionally a passing neighbor would visit for a moment, sometimes leaving a bunch of flowers and sometimes a prayer that God would support me in my affliction. One dark night there came up a very great storm of wind and rain. The lightning flashed constantly and the thunder shook my cabin until I certainly thought it would fall down. Being all alone my fears were great. But all at once a light, beautiful and soft, filled all the room, and I thought I heard a voice whisper saying, 'Be not afraid, I am with you, you shall not be afraid of the terror by night.' Suddenly I seemed to see the presence of shining ones in my room. I sat up in my bed and said, 'Oh, Lord, are You here?' and repeated a word from the prophet: 'I will trust and not be afraid, for the Lord Jehovah is my strength and my song.' (Isaiah 12:2) All the remainder of that night I was filled with praises to God. My soul was exceedingly happy."

Just then the angel who had been talking with us, smilingly said, "I know all about that night and was present with you. I was present also at your bedside the night you died and strengthened your soul that your trust might be perfect until you were released, and my co-charioteer over there brought you safely to the portals of paradise." Just at this moment she began to praise God again for her great deliverance, and I said to myself again, 'Surely those who had the poorest and hardest fare in the world are happiest now.'

We have lingered long enough just for a glance at the surroundings outside the city walls. I must hurry on to what was within, for great attractions were inside. [d]

* * *

We were nearing the great gateway. Every one of the new arrivals was filled with wonder and excitement. We had heard so much about the holy city while we lived in the world, of its many mansions, its streets of gold, its gates of pearl, its transparent light without sun or moon, so that we all felt an intense yearning to enter in. But the greatest attraction of all was to see Him whom our souls loved and by whom we had been redeemed and by whose blood we had been washed from our sins. We had already been told that He was waiting near the gate in one of the mansions and that the great Book of Life would be near Him and be opened to the pages bearing our names. This filled us with great anxiety—although we felt a sweet assurance that our names were there, and that we would receive His gracious welcome. Yes, we felt sure or we never would have been carried by the angels into paradise were it not so. For we had confessed Him on earth and we knew He had already confessed us before His Father and the angels. This gave us comfort, and then we knew we had been eating of the tree of life and drinking of the crystal river, so with confidence we kept looking forward. We knew we had been trying to please Him, and the conscious sense that all our sin had been forgiven and our robes washed and made white was additional consolation to us now. We felt we would soon stand before the Judge of all the earth.

God's Word seemed further comfort where He says: "Blessed are they that do His commandments, that they may have right to the tree of life, and may enter in through the gates into the city." (Revelation 22:14) We felt such a comfort in this assurance, that if we had a right to the tree of life, and the fruit given us was by an elder's hand, and that Abraham himself had refreshed and immortalized us from the river of God which came from the Throne itself, that the angel at the gate would not prevent us from entering now.

Just at this time my mother, who had been busily engaged in conversation with others, came to me and said, "You need have no fears. It gave me much joy when many years ago I was passing near where the angel was recording the names of those who had been born again, and seeing your name I at once asked the angel who it was. He called another angel who had just come from the scenes of earthly conflict, where they were having great religious awakenings, and asked him if he could tell who these were whose names were just written. 'Oh,' he said, 'I have just been among them,' and described everything in such detail that I had all assurance it was you. Then other names which I saw registered were from the same place. My old home—our old home. Indeed the memory of it is dear to me as I think of it now. We will talk over the details of it someday, as things have been since I left you all. My soul was filled with exceeding great joy when I saw your name. Then the angel told me when he found I was your mother, that he went with you and your cousin, whom I knew so well, one night as you went from the scenes of prayer and stood by your side late at night, while you solemnly made a vow and pledged faithfulness to God and to each other, that he went and woke your father who was sleeping in another room and led him out to witness your covenant. Oh, you may know that not only I, but the angels rejoiced with me when they brought me the news. He also told me of the conversion of other members of our family, and many more in the neighborhood."

"Well, well," I said, "does heaven have such communications as these with the affairs of the world?" How little we seemed to know it! Yet my mother's words brought up all this past experience. The scenes of my conversion, midnight prayers, earnest labor for others, the events she just alluded to with many others all came rushing through my mind and the memory was fresh as though but yesterday.

I said, "How blind I was not to see the angel who was with me. The mighty veil of mortality, how it blinds the eye of man from spiritual beings and things! How far away they seem to be and yet how very near! I remembered how angels assisted Lot and his family from the condemned city of Sodom, and why should they not assist in the soul's great struggle after salvation! For I remember: 'They are all ministering spirits sent forth to minister for those who shall be heirs of salvation.'" (Hebrews 1:14)

By this time we were entering the massive Judean gateway. Our hearts were all filled with joy in the expectation of so soon seeing Him whom our souls loved. As we passed through the gateway the most beautiful scene met our gaze that we had ever witnessed before in heaven or on earth. Human language cannot describe it. To say the streets were pure gold or transparent glass

would give the best idea by way of comparison of any objec.
know. The great thoroughfares leading from the gate seemed
to lead off toward the center of the holy city. On the right hand
as we passed in were mighty, stupendous columns of precious
stone shining with a brightness that heaven only knows. Massive
domes and great archways were overhead. Nothing showed
any signs of decay or age. No rubbish or signs of wear. The light
toward the mansions was exceeding great. Our Lord now came
forward to meet and welcome us. Twelve legions of happy souls
had now filed in at the great gateway and stood before our King.
The glory and majesty of His being can never be described. The
beloved disciple on Patmos once tried to tell of His glorious
appearance as He revealed Himself on earth. He was then
clothed with a flowing garment down to His feet and girt about
with a golden belt. His head and hair seemed white as snow, and
His eyes as a flame of fire. His feet were glowing like burnished
brass. His countenance was like the sun at midday, a sharp two-
edged sword was in his mouth and seven stars were in His right
hand. (Revelation 1:13-16) But when the disciples saw Him on the
Mount of Transfiguration sixty-three years before, His garments
then shone as the light and His face with the brilliancy of the
sun. On earth He was called the fairest among ten thousand
and altogether lovely. But as He is now in His exaltation in
heaven—the language is too tame to express His glory. He bore
the marks in His hands, and above His sandals the nail prints
showed distinctly. He was the very embodiment of light. It was
not dazzling to our eyes as was Moses' face to Israel of old, for
we were prepared for it—since the days of our conversion on
earth until we passed through this gate we were being prepared
for this vision of our Lord. Oh, how powerful were the words of
Scripture as I looked upon His face and then glanced far into the
city! "And the city had no need of the sun, neither of the moon,
for the glory of God did lighten it and the Lamb is the light
thereof." (Revelation 21:23) He was also the embodiment of love
itself. Every feature of His face spoke of love. Indeed it was the
reflection of His Father's infinite love. All the love in heaven or
in the church on earth came from Him. He welcomed us to Him,
and as we came, by one mighty impulse we all fell on our faces

and began to worship Him with adoring praise, saying, "Worthy is the Lamb that was slain and has redeemed us to God by your blood out of every kindred and tongue and people and nation." (Revelation 5:9) The angels and the saints who met us, also joined and sang some new songs which we had never heard before. Our souls were in ecstasies of joy not to be described.

How long we remained upon our faces we could not tell for our gladness, joys and great satisfaction were so deep and blessed we took no note of eternity's register. He now addressed us in most loving words, giving us His cordial welcome and confessing us before the multitude of angels present, and to His Father's face, and without further introduction we felt perfectly acquainted.

"Come," said He, "look into this Book. I have opened it to the pages most interesting to you."

We all gathered around Him in turns as closely as we could, to look upon the pages of the great Book of books, the heavenly records of the past and future.

Not only were our names written, but underneath them were many things bearing upon our work for God while in the earth. I then remembered what God had said by one of His prophets which I read a hundred times over. That a, "book of remembrance was written before Him for them that thought upon His name, 'And they shall be mine,' saith the Lord of hosts, 'in that day when I make up my jewels.'" (Malachi 3:16-17)

We only took time to read a little of what was written, for our Lord said, "You now have perfect liberty to go where you will and to read at your leisure the contents of this most wonderful book." In glancing over its pages we noticed the names of some who were with us when we first entered paradise, who had fallen back in the rear and remained far outside the gates of pearl. Without any further words of explanation we knew that they were not prepared, but were like the ancient high priest when unsanctified, unworthy of the altar, so these could not serve around the Throne. Yet we knew they would be brought in, for they were somewhere along the river of life and among the trees whose fruit was their food and whose leaves were for their healing. Their present reward was all that God could give them with their present stage of grace. These leaves, we knew, were only for those whose names were in the Book of Life and that they have the same healing power in them that the sanctifying grace of God had in His kingdom on earth. The remedy indeed was around them, but they would not receive it. They never realized the deep meaning of the precious sacrifice for them, but how thankful to know that the power of His blood is so effective for those of His people on this side of the river as well as on that. We knew also that much of our redemption is yet to follow and will be realized at the resurrection morning of the great day.

I had often wondered if we should have knowledge of the lost ones and should miss any of our friends from the holy city, if we would not be filled with sadness and grief, although God had said: "All tears should be wiped away." (Revelation 21:4) But now I found it was all settled; I had been there long enough to pass the river of life, drink of its crystal waters, eat of the fruit of the trees upon its banks, and be greeted by thousands of the blood-washed from the chariots of God, beside entering in at the gates, and during all this time only the highest emotions of praise filled my soul. I was so completely in God's love, and my own will was so lost in the conscious will of my blessed Redeemer, that I had never thought once of weeping about anything. In fact, I found that all my faculties and inclination to sorrow and sadness were gone and I could see things as God sees them.

And then as I stood beside my Redeemer and Lord, and the great Book of Life lay open before me, and I could see far into the city and could see multitudes of happy souls whom I had not met nor did I know who they might be—some I did not know, but some whom I had known on earth and had feared were among the lost might be here in the city, and especially since I had been greeted by some whom I never expected to see in heaven. And in looking over the pages of the Book of Life I saw the names of many whom I thought would not be there, and I knew they must be somewhere in the great city or in the vast domains of the paradise of God.

I now felt eager to go on and mingle with the happy souls which I saw passing in all directions. The Lord had said, "You have entire liberty. Go where you will." I turned to see the rest of our legions, for I had been so enraptured by what I saw and heard, that I had stayed long, but to my surprise they had scattered in many directions—some had gone with their friends to quiet places, and beneath the trees, they were sitting on the upholstery of heaven in joyous conversation; others, meeting with old friends, had boarded the chariots and with them gone to distant places of the city.

My mother was still near me and motioned for me to come with her. We walked only a short distance and sat down beside a stupendous column of what seemed jasper and sapphire, shining with the light which the eternal city only knows. The cushions were of the finest fabric, and the upholstering had been done by the hands of saints and angels, for everyone is busily employed in heaven. Compulsion is not known, but contentment of which we only knew the shadow while in our most restful moments in earth, seemed to clothe everyone here as a garment. [e]

* * *

I now turned to my mother and said, "I have been wanting a private talk with you for some time. It does seem so good to be here with you. It seems like a very short time since I sat upon your knee and you told me the story of our future home. How little I comprehended the reality of it! But we are safe in the city now and I want to ask you some questions about our home here, our privileges and duties."

"Be perfectly free to ask any questions you like. We learn of the wonders of our Father's house, just as we did on earth, by applying ourselves to all the means and sources of knowledge."

"I want to know first what privileges we have here in heaven, both in the city and outside in paradise and elsewhere, and what are the laws that govern these privileges and our behavior?"

"I understand fully," she said, "what you want to know. You have asked some very important questions, and I am glad to assist you with any detailed explanations you wish.

"Your privileges, however, are unbounded. Your capacities for pleasure and enjoyment are greatly enlarged since leaving the scenes of your earthly life. Everything here invites the fullest exercise of every faculty of your soul. Your behavior will be governed by a knowledge of God's will. You will never wish to do anything or act in any way contrary to the will of God.

"The law of love and light is the law of the heavenly kingdom. No one wishes to do anything here which would not be morally right. There is no thought or suggestion by anyone, of himself or another doing anything morally wrong. You have found, no doubt, before this that you have no inclinations within yourself or temptation from without to do any wrong thing. Everything that you feel inclined to do is right, so far as moral right is concerned. Your knowledge is yet limited. Whatever God approves and your knowledge comprehends, you will approve from the innermost depths of your soul. His will becomes law to you. He never charges guilt upon anyone here, for no one in all this heavenly kingdom has any feelings or wish to disobey. Sin is not known here. That great curse of the earth is entirely banished from these streets and mansions of the city, from the drives, walks and resorts of paradise as well. No stain of sin has ever been here since God cast out the angels who sinned. Every one of those thousands whom you see over there coming and going are the image of God so completely that they have no desire to do otherwise than just to fulfill His will. Our duty here is only a blessed privilege. It is our great delight to do all we ought to do. Restraint and compulsion, of which I remember we knew so much in the earth, are words which have no meaning here. You have noticed, no doubt before this, that everyone you have met or seen has been perfectly joyful and happy. Discontent is unknown here. Everyone is altogether satisfied and entirely at rest."

"Oh, how wonderfully grand this is!" I replied. "But I should like to know further, if I do not weary you with my questions, what privileges we have here in heaven, by way of going from place to place, and visiting among the beautiful mansions I see lining those great avenues and thoroughfares of the city. Our Lord has said, 'Go where you will, enjoy yourselves.'"

"Oh!" she said, smilingly. "Go just where you please. All that you see and infinitely more are yours—yes, all are yours. Do you not remember that Scripture: 'All are yours, and ye are Christ's and Christ is God's'? (1 Corinthians 3:22-23) I have been here for over sixty years and I have gone multitudes of times to distant parts of the city, and yet I have seen but a little portion of my inheritance. Speaking in language which you will better understand, the city is fifteen hundred miles each way and its height is the same as its length and breadth. (Revelation 21:16-17) So its vastness is sufficient for you and you have the privileges of it all."

"Oh, my mother! How wonderful are the works of God! I am simply lost in admiration and wonder!"

"Indeed," said she, "your wonder will never come to an end. Story upon story is built and the inconceivable height and glory and vastness can never be fully comprehended by us. You see those fountains over there gushing with their pure water of life?"

"Yes," I replied, "I have been noticing them for quite a while and wanted to ask you concerning them, for I see so many gathering about them and drinking from golden goblets. I presume they are free for all?"

"Indeed, and they are throughout the city and even to the remotest parts of paradise. Do you remember the Scripture which I used to read to you nearly seventy years ago, that, 'The Lamb which is in the midst of the Throne shall feed them and shall lead them unto living fountains of waters'?" (Revelation 7:17)

"Sure enough, I have read it hundreds of times since, but I never thought it meant so much."

"But when you get to the Throne itself you will see the greatness of its meaning as you cannot now. You have already eaten of the trees of life, and drank of the crystal river, I am sure, for you have that privilege immediately on coming into the border lands of heaven, but did you notice there were twelve kinds of fruit on each tree?" (Revelation 22:2)

"Yes, so the elder told me. I have eaten only a very few times since entering paradise, and others have selected for me. Those lovely trees in the midst of the street, how full of fruit they are!"

"They were all planted and are growing by the immediate direction of our Lord Himself," said mother. "You remember His words while on earth: 'I go to prepare a place for you,' (John 14:2) and here it is. Those fountains and trees with all their blessing are forever yours. One never tires of anything he has here, nor wishes for anything that he cannot have. The varieties of food are so abundant you can eat and be wholly satisfied."

Just at this moment we saw one not far away, whom among the thousands we distinguished as one of the elders. I said to mother, "Would he mind stopping for a short visit with us? What do you think?"

"No doubt he would be pleased to do so." So she motioned for him to come over to us. As he was coming toward us she said, "Oh, it is Moses, sure."

"How thankful I am," I replied, "for I have been wishing to see him ever since we entered paradise." But as he came nearer I felt something of an awe coming over me as I remembered his greatness while on earth. I also felt a fear that the questions which I wished to ask him might not interest him since, as I thought, he had been asked the same a thousand times.

"You don't need to fear," said mother, "to ask him any questions you like, for he will take great pleasure in assisting you in any way he can."

Meeting a group at one of the fountains nearby, he was detained for a time, in conversation with them. While waiting for him, I said, "I remember in the Scriptures it is said, 'There are twenty-four elders in heaven.'"

"Yes," said mother, "twelve from former dispensations and twelve since the days of Christ."

I asked if there were the same distinctions and reverence shown here as on earth.

"Quite the same," said she, "only on a true basis—for past fidelity and merit. The elders are greatly honored here in heaven. They have already had their resurrection which gives them superior advantages for enjoyment and service and yet their bodies are so spiritual that instead of being a hindrance to them they are a very great help and advantage. You have noticed, no doubt, how wonderfully they are in the likeness of the Lord Himself."

"I have noticed that already in what I have seen in Abraham and Joshua, and I now remember that Scripture where the prophet said, 'I shall be satisfied when I awake in your likeness.'" (Psalm 17:15)

"Indeed," said mother, "and we are all looking toward that event with great interest. No doubt you have heard since your coming that the Lord has intimated that the time has nearly come when the general resurrection will take place. When you and I and all these multitudes of souls shall have our spiritual bodies. The great Father Himself, whose Spirit you so abundantly feel and which is the very atmosphere of the city and all paradise, has made us all to feel and know that the time is nearly here. There are some events to occur upon earth first, and then our Lord Jesus accompanied with all the angels and this mighty host of redeemed spirits made perfect, will descend to the earth, the order will be that when we are near the earth where our bodies are sleeping (for what we used to call death is only a sleep), that the archangel will give a great shout of victory and the trumpet of God will be blown with a mighty blast and the power of God will awaken and revive all our bodies and they will instantly spring from the dust and with a mighty change will be made spiritual and we will instantly be united with them and be forever in the perfect image of Jesus, and the last stroke of our redemption will be completed."

"Oh!" I replied. "How wonderful is the plan of our redemption! God has given us, I remember, the same idea of what you have been saying as recorded in the New Testament Scripture."

"Yes," said mother, "and this is the hope and expectation of all the church in heaven and on earth. But I see Moses is now coming to us and we will have to leave further conversation on this subject until another time."

CHAPTER FOUR
Meeting Moses

y this time he had come to us, and with a friendly greeting we shook hands and my mother gave us an introduction. He very cordially welcomed me, and in a moment all my feelings of backwardness at meeting with such an honored and favored servant of God as he had been and was were gone. The grace with which he met me and the welcome he gave caused an immediate yearning in me to be near him. I felt I could lean my head with great joy on his bosom.

The meekness so characteristic of his nature while on earth clothed every feature of his soul now. He did not seem like a man who had lived one hundred twenty years on the earth under such great burdens of responsibilities as he had passed through. There were no marks of age, or wrinkles or any oldish looking appearance about him. Only his hair and beard were of flaxen whiteness. He was rather above the average in stature, and his robes were white as snow. He stood quite erect and had a most imposing dignity and yet so gentle and lovely that my soul loved him exceedingly at once.

My mother and he entered into a short conversation about a number of children who were just outside the gate, and asked me to excuse their conversation a moment. I heard him ask her if she would go and assist them in the knowledge and ways of the heavenly kingdom. We were so near the gateway, that we could distinctly hear them singing and could discern the voices—very sweet and angelic. Mother said she would be quite glad to go and spend some time among them and teach them of heavenly things. So turning to Moses she said, "My son would be pleased for a short visit with you, as he has only recently entered the city."

"I shall be much pleased also," said Moses, "for to assist and help each other is much of our occupation in heaven as you know yourself."

Whereupon my mother made a gentle bow, adding the words, "I'll see you again," and waving a good-bye with her hand she was gone.

Moses now said, "You were fortunate to have had such a mother on earth. She is greatly esteemed in heaven, and very much used in the service of her Lord. But I see, my son, you are very full of questions and the inquiries and investigations of your soul are of great service to you here. Let us walk to that cluster of trees over there and take some fruit that we may be eat while we talk. I always enjoyed the social and religious feasts while on earth, and it remains with me still. I greatly enjoy eating with my friends." He selected from the different kinds what we wanted and said as he handed me a bunch of what seemed like large transparent grapes. These will help you in understanding the mystery of the kingdom of God—mysteries not so much connected with our redemption as our further development in heaven and growth in a knowledge of His will for the great future."

"There have been great discussions of recent years," I said to Moses, "over some portions of the Scripture, especially of the book of Genesis which you wrote, what was meant and what time embraced in the six days of creation, and the seventh day in which it is said, 'God rested.' I used to say if ever I got to heaven I would see Moses and ask about these things. And at last, here we are, face to face."

"Well," said Moses, "my time and knowledge are at your disposal. I have been asked very similar questions hundreds of times. But just one word of explanation will make it all clear to you. In the first place, to begin back of where I began when writing under the inspiration of God, before the beginning the great cycles of eternity knew nothing of the earth. It was known *re giving & receiving* "it is My law"

only in the mind of God, and long before He laid the foundations of the earth, He thought of each of us. But this beginning and each successive day of creation were long periods of time. Each cycle was called a day which measured a vast period of creation under infinite laws. The same laws were in operation as they are now—God's will was simply His law. When He said, 'Let the dry land appear,' ages were occupied in developing the continents for our earthly home, and so period after period, the work was done and the earth was populated with creation of His own will. Great events are in store for the earth yet. The restitution of all things has not occurred yet. God shall cleanse, change and remodel it again by fire. His voice shall yet shake the earth as it has never been shaken. He shall prepare it for a suitable place for His bride in the great wedding tour which we will yet take. Do you not remember His Word, written long after my day: 'Whose voice then shook the earth, but now He has promised saying, "Yet once more I will shake not the earth only but also heaven"'? (Hebrews 12:26) The renovation of the earth and the removing out of His kingdom there all things which offend and do iniquity is another great day yet to come, and nearly here. All the wise ones of earth will be ready and waiting for it."

"Well," I said to Moses, "I am deeply interested in these great matters of creation, but may we not leave them for another visit for there are other things which I wish to ask you about."

"Certainly," said Moses.

"Tell me something concerning our Lord Jesus, before He was born in the world and became our sacrifice for sin."

"Well," said Moses, "He was always one with the Father. He was truly the Word of God. The creative energy of the almighty Jehovah. Without Him God did nothing. 'Let us make,' was an expression common in all the works and creations of God. His title always was the 'Word,' and until He was born on earth He was not known as the Son, but as the Word only. He has been present in the creation of the world, and was and is the glory of the Father's Throne in this celestial kingdom. But it was a great event in heaven when the announcement was made that Jesus was born in Bethlehem. It was the most exciting occasion ever witnessed in all the heavenly domain. All the angels tuned their harps, for the Lord said, 'Let all the angels of God worship Him.' I have seen great times on earth when the millions of Israel all joined in the chorus of praise at the passage of the Red Sea, and when all the great hosts rushed from their tents at the sounding of the trumpet of God on Mount Sinai, but never was anything equal to this. Multitudes of angels at once descended to where the infant Jesus was, but no such worship or music has ever been heard in heaven. Everything throughout all the streets and avenues of the city and even to the utmost bounds of paradise the voice of thanksgiving was being poured forth to God. The angels were not alone in this praise, for all of us who had come from the earth knew that our salvation was through Him who had just been born into the world and you may know we all joined with them in one prolonged praise to God. It was an event which had been pondered with great interest by all the heavenly host for long ages past."

"Thank God," I said to Moses, "for His birth. And I now remember a passage of the blessed word of the Lord bearing on this same subject: 'Of which salvation the prophets have enquired and searched diligently who prophesied of the grace that should come unto you. Searching what or what manner of time, the Spirit of God which was in them did signify when it testified beforehand the sufferings of Christ and the glory that should follow: Unto whom it was revealed that not unto themselves, but unto us, they did minister the things which are now reported unto you, by them that have preached the gospel unto you with the Holy Ghost sent down from heaven, which things the angels desire to look into.'" (1 Peter 1:10-12)

"You are right, my son," said Moses, "and we all knew that the world's redemption was connected with His birth, life and death. The angels were in constant attendance upon Him at all times and brought us detailed accounts of all that occurred in His life. Many things of which I am told there is no record upon earth are faithfully written in the Book of Life, a volume of which is at each of the twelve gates and the angel always has charge of it. If you desire," said Moses, "we will walk at once to the Judean gateway, which is not far from here and see some of the things written therein."

I said to him, "I entered at that gate only a short time ago and saw the Book and glanced over a few of its pages and should be much pleased to look into it again, for our Lord said, 'You can all read at your leisure.'"

As we were going, Moses said to me, "Did the Book meet your expectations?"

"Oh," I said, "it far exceeded them. It is so large and grand, yet it seemed easily handled, for everything in heaven seems to be of such a spiritual character."

He quickly turned to that portion bearing the title, "Records of the Son of God." As he slowly turned the pages I glanced at the various headings bearing on the many events in His most wonderful life. It was exceedingly interesting and precious to notice with what wonderful harmony the records of His life were given in the Scriptures and in this blessed Book of all books. It seemed more interesting still, since I knew that one had been written by the instrumentality of man and the other by the hand of angels. The angels know all about our language and have written all things intelligible to us. The angels whom Jacob saw in his dream ascending and descending upon the ladder, bearing confirmations of the covenant given to Abraham were the same who were in constant attendance upon the Son of God during His wonderful incarnate life upon earth, and watched every detail of His life, and much of it has been faithfully written. I read with fresh interest the account of His birth, of the special illumination by the guiding star given to the wise men of the east, in the language of the Record, "A light from heaven guided them to the place where the world's Redeemer was born." Of Herod's miserable attempt to destroy Him by killing all the young children of those parts, and of his continued and determined wrath against Him until an angel brought his life to an end.

As he turned the pages I noticed many accounts of His early life not given in the Scriptures. One especially attracted my attention, the title was, "Jesus Taught by the Father." The event seemed to occur when He was but five years old. Joseph had gone from home and the child Jesus was left alone in His father's place of business, His mother being busy in the house. Suddenly a bright cloud filled all that mechanic's room. The Father Himself overshadowed and held conversation with Him, telling Him who He was: that God was His Father, and communicated to Him much concerning His earthly mission. "All this," said Moses, "he knew as God, but as He was man also He learned by being taught."

Another account was written, "Caught Up to Paradise." It was during the night while all were asleep that He was caught up to the paradise of God and was with the Father for many hours in which the Father said to Him, "You are man as well as God for you were born of a woman. All power and authority shall soon be given into Your hands, and You shall lay down Your life for the salvation of men." I then quickly remembered His own words: "This commandment I have received from my Father." (John 10:18) "You shall also prepare and fix up mansions in this upper kingdom for Your future home and that of all Your children for they shall be many."

Before morning had broken upon the earth, angels had returned Him safely to His home at Nazareth and before any stir by servants or parents He was in His room in prayer.

"Now," said Moses, "this incarnate life of Jesus on earth was made necessary on account of man's sin and rebellion against God. No other method was ever devised for our salvation. You can look further into the book if you like, and at any time you wish."

* * *

"These accounts," I replied, "are exceedingly interesting. I have often said while on earth that many things we did not know, nor could know, we would know hereafter."

"True enough," said Moses. "The fact is, we only just began to know the first elementary principles of the knowledge of God while on earth."

"I suppose that would be true of the large mass of mankind whose knowledge is so limited concerning divine things, but you seem to include yourself along with the rest of us, and it seems a little strange since you were for so many years in such intimate fellowship with God—talked face to face with Him—saw His glory so often, were His special friend so long."

"I know," said Moses, "that God did highly favor me, but it was for your sakes as much as my own, but after all, since I came into the heavenly kingdom and into His immediate presence about the Throne, I find I know but little of what is evidently yet to be known. God revealed much of Himself to me, as I thought, but that much was only a little of the great mysteries of His eternal nature, wisdom and works. Even as regards our common salvation, the angels who for long ages have been about the Throne, are yet eager to learn. Here," said Moses, "is a page you would like to see, I am sure. It is one of the great events in the earlier life of Jesus, not recorded in the Holy Scriptures on earth."

The headlines were, "The mission of Jesus more fully confirmed by the Father." The event occurred when He was about twenty-two years of age. He had retired to a distant mountain to pray and was all alone, except many of the angels were about Him, when the Father in a most extraordinary manner met with Him and reiterated in fullness of meaning all that had been revealed by the shadows of the law. The Father spoke of His death to be accomplished at Jerusalem and of its vicarious nature—how His death was to be for all men and showed Him the fullness of His love for the world, and that His sufferings and death should be the price of the world's redemption, and that His death should be the great atonement for the salvation of man. The account also showed how He should die and the awful sorrows of the occasion: His rejection by the Jews, His scourging and final death on the cross. Reference was also made of His resurrection and ascension into heaven. "All these things," said Moses, "Jesus as the Word always knew, but as the Son of God, He was instructed by the Father, and fully did His will in all His incarnate life on earth."

Very many things I saw written there of the occurrences in His life were most interesting to me now. "Oh, yes," I replied to Moses as he turned the pages, "I remember how John the beloved disciple said as he finished his narrative of the Son of God: 'And there are many other things which Jesus did, the which if they should be written every one, I suppose that even the world itself could not contain the books that should be written.'" (John 21:25)

I asked Moses why these are written here instead of in the records on earth.

"These," he replied, "are for the satisfaction and comfort of God's children in heaven."

"Well, well," I remarked, "I am lost in wonder and surprise. But, father Moses," I said, "you had a most remarkable experience in the days of our Lord while on earth. The Scriptures make reference to the transfiguration of Jesus on the Holy Mount and that He took Peter, James and John with Him and that you and Elijah came also and were talking with Him concerning His death."

"Yes," said Moses, "I look back to that event with great pleasure. At the time the hosts of Israel were ready to cross the Jordan into the land of their inheritance I was very eager to go over with them, but God thought it not best, and His will is always right. I did not then know that He meant to answer my prayer after so many long years had passed—that is, long years as regards earthly count—it was only a day and a half of heaven's measure.

"That was a great day when the Lord summoned us to the earth. All powers had just been given into His hands both in heaven and in earth. I cannot fully describe to you our feelings when Elijah and myself were walking together near the Throne talking of the great event so soon to occur in the earth, and its great meaning both to earth and heaven. I was speaking of His tragic death soon to be accomplished on the cross, and He of the blessed gift of the Holy Ghost to be offered to all God's children on the earth—for our great mission and concern had been to unfold these two features of the work of the Son of God.

We had enjoyed many precious visits and much conversation about these questions when unexpectedly Michael, one of the chief angels, whom possibly you have seen, and Jehuco, the swift charioteer, brought a chariot to our side and said that we were called for immediately to the earth. Without further preparations we were quickly seated by their side and, with almost the speed of thought, we were flying through the great avenues and passed out of the city at the gate of Manasseh. The vast plains, mountains and valleys of paradise were quickly passed. We were so enraptured with the thought of a visit to earth we hardly knew what to say nor had we time to say it until we were slowing down somewhere in the regions of a terrestrial sphere. In a moment more, its cities, towns, mountains and rivers were visible to us. Just at this moment Michael said to Jehuco, 'Reduce your speed still more and drive the chariot past Mount Nebo.' I exclaimed and said, 'Oh, Michael, you blessed servant of God. Are we so near the land of my earthly pilgrimage, and to the mount where my last earthly prayer was offered and where I laid aside the veil of my flesh? I am so glad to see old Nebo again. My body was laid away somewhere here.' 'Yes,' said Michael, 'we know all about it and where it is. I will speak unto you again later on about it, but now we must hurry on.' In a moment more the chariot wheels were standing still on Olivet's summit, and we had stepped upon the earth which had been the scenes of my former life and within the promised land to which I had led the host of Israel, and so strongly desired to enter it myself, and now my prayer was answered after many hundreds of years had passed.

* * *

Moses continued and said, "Only a short distance from us was a bright cloud suspended a little way above, but really it was settling down upon the mount. It reminded me very much of the cloud that went before us in the wilderness and led the hosts of Israel in their journeys. We quickly left the chariot and the angels standing by its side, and proceeded to the place over which the cloud hung. As we came near we had the first glimpse of Him who was both God and man. He had clothed Himself in the garments of heaven for the occasion. We found Him on His knees in prayer and somewhat hidden behind some low shrubbery. The three disciples were kneeling near Him, but were so overcome with the glory that they seemed asleep. He arose and met us with a most cordial greeting, and the place was so resplendent with glory that it seemed we might have been still about the Throne itself. It did seem a little strange to think we were upon the earth again. We knew the time had arrived when He should become the great sacrifice for the world's redemption. I had foreshadowed Him by the manifold shadows of the law. Indeed, I saw something of His majesty and the glory of His kingdom when in a figure God made my face to shine like the sun on Mount Sinai, with which, no doubt, you are familiar, for it was faithfully written." (Exodus 34:29)

"Oh! I remember it quite well," I replied, "and have often made reference to it as typifying the beauty of moral character."

"Very true," said Moses, "but it also foreshadowed the transfiguration scene and the future period yet to come, and which, we are informed is near at hand, when the millennial glory of Christ is to appear upon the earth and all the saints shall share in the glory, a glimpse of which was seen on the Holy Mount.

"We stood united in our testimony to the Son of God. But after we had been called away the three disciples saw no man but Jesus only. The great Father spoke out of the cloud and declared this was His only beloved Son, well pleasing to Him. We had much conversation with Him on the great themes of sacrifice and atonement, the Holy Spirit, and the plan of man's redemption. The church now has ample proof of His divinity and can fully trust in the great sacrifice which He has made.

"Our Lord spoke as familiarly to me as though we had been intimately acquainted for hundreds of years, and indeed He had been during much of my earthly life and toil, my constant friend. He was the 'Angel of the Covenant,' and was in the cloud which went before and followed us in our journeys in the wilderness. Long before His incarnation in the flesh He was the light of heaven and was with His church on earth. He gave us a cordial introduction to the disciples with whom we spoke.

"When He had dismissed us, the chariot drove to our side, and in a few moments we said good-bye, and leaving Olivet's summit were on our homeward trip. Michael now turned to me and said, 'Would you like to go past the cave?' 'I should be greatly delighted,' I replied, 'will you please stop a moment at its threshold?'

"When the chariot stood still, Michael, Elijah and myself stepped out. Michael now said, 'No man has known where your body was laid until this day. The Lord directed a secret burial, lest the people of Israel should worship your remains. The devil contended for a long time that we should give it a public burial. But you are aware that we are now at the place? Your body was laid far back in a cave that used to be here. After it had been laid to rest, we touched the rocks and they came down and filled the entrance and here it has been sleeping ever since.' At this I humbly bowed myself before God and blessed Him for His promise of the resurrection.

"We now quickly ascended to the top of Pisgah and once again I was standing where I had stood nearly sixteen hundred years before. Oh, how fresh the memories of it all were! Everything came back to me."

I had been so entranced by this remarkable story, that I almost thought myself on the earth again, but turning to Moses, I said, "How wonderful are the dealings of God to the children of men! What great things are in store for them!"

"Surely," said Moses, "but I must finish my narrative. Just here Michael said, 'We must hurry on.' Seated again in the chariot he said to his charioteer, 'Go past Bethlehem, for there are two souls just released which we must take with us.' The chariot seemed to go with the speed of lightning. We received the two souls and were soaring to the regions above and toward the gateways of paradise. When we had stepped out, Elijah remained with them for further instruction, and I was soon once more at the Throne.

"I see," said Moses, "that we have been standing here a long time and you will have ample time to look into this Book at your leisure."

"I am thankful for that," I replied, "and shall often take advantage of the privilege."

Moses now said, "You have not been far into the city, nor about the Throne, have you?"

"No, but I am eager to go, if I only had someone to go with me as a guide. There were many who entered the city at the same time I did, but they have all disappeared among the countless crowds I see in every direction."

"You have taken a wise course, my son. Get acquainted as you go along. There are many who will lend you all the assistance you require. I see you are eager to see your mother again, she will return to you soon and you can enjoy her company as you will."

"I thank you very much for your kindness, father Moses, and will make the most of the opportunities as they come to me."

Moses then said, "I hope to see you again soon, and at the Throne if not before," and with a pleasant word of blessing he said good-bye.

I turned around only to see my friend Bohemond coming toward me. We had parted at the Judean gate and had not met since. So we went to a quiet place and sat down to talk over the things of our wonderful visits and experiences.

CHAPTER FIVE
A Great Prayer Meeting in Heaven

ohemond and I now walked a short distance to a most remarkable cluster of buildings which Moses had just pointed out to me. They were massive, stupendous, and grand. They occupied one whole block of the city and seemed to be foursquare. A great inscription was written above the threshold, "Treasures laid Up in Heaven."

We spent a long time going from place to place looking into these wonderful treasures, which God's people have secured for themselves, as well as rejected blessings which might have been secured by diligent effort while on earth, for we found that all these multitudes of holy gems, jewels, pearls and lovely garments all had their counterpart in the experience of saints on earth. These heavenly jewels might have been easily secured and would have added much to the riches of the soul in the heavenly kingdom. But I can tell you more of these at another time. Before leaving the Shrine of Holy Symbols we were told that not far away from here was a place where great congregations meet for public worship and praise, many hundreds of which are located in different parts of the holy city. I said to Bohemond, "Let us go there at once for we have enjoyed no congregational worship since leaving the Judean gate."

As we stepped out at the door of the sacred shrine onto the opened street we found it was literally crowded with thousands of happy souls on their way to the great praise service. "Oh,

65

listen," I said to Bohemond, "to the strains of music." It seemed far in the distance and yet we could hear it quite distinctly.

"Oh," he replied to me, "it must be the orchestra of heaven."

"Indeed, I think it is, and I am eager to be among them." I spoke to one of the many who were crowding the streets and who seemed to be perfectly acquainted with the surroundings, asking if he could tell about the order of the service and the chances of a convenient place.

"To be sure," said he, "every comfort is provided. Have you not attended the service before?"

"This is our first, as we have just recently come into the city,"

"Then you will be welcomed and ushered to a more prominent place, so you will have better opportunities of learning the worship of heaven. All the strangers are brought forward and introduced to the great multitudes and given favored places. So you will be entirely free and easy."

We thanked him for his kindness and felt a sense of relief.

Just at this point came two chariots sweeping along in which were seated many of the patriarchs, prophets, and apostles of Jesus. I noticed that each of them had a harp, and someone with a large stringed instrument stood up prominently among them. I said, "Who is the man with his face shining with such glory, having the stringed instrument?"

Several spoke at once and said, "You have sung his hymns and Psalms a thousand times. Guess who he is."

I did not need to be told. I knew it was David the King. Anticipating my desires someone motioned to the charioteer. David also called us to come and sit with him. We were soon by his side and the chariot was rolling along with noiseless but reduced speed. I said to David and the rest, as I turned toward my friend, "This is Bohemond from northern Russia whom I met at my first introduction into paradise. I am from the opposite side of the earth, and although our homes were so remote from each other, yet we are brethren in the Lord."

"We are glad to welcome you, my sons, to the holy city, and also into this chariot," said David. "Of course, you are going where we all are going, up to join the great congregation in the worship and praise of our Redeemer?"

"Indeed we are and shall be glad to go along with you, for we know but little of the order of worship here."

"Just that which springs up in your souls is most pleasing to God. I see you have your harps with you. Have you learned to use them?"

"Oh, yes, and I have been practicing some new hymns we sang at our entrance into paradise and at the gate of the city. We used to sing your Psalms of praise on earth, as well as the song of Moses, but when I heard the first strain of music in heaven I concluded we did not know how to sing at all."

"Oh, well," said David, "you will have no trouble in joining in with the music here. Do you not hear the orchestra now? We shall all join them soon."

I had been so entranced at our situation and surroundings and so absorbed in the conversation that I had almost forgotten who or where I was, but turning to Bohemond, I said, "How blessed to be here, and then, just to think, we are with the old prophets of God of whom we have read so much!"

At this Bohemond again fell on his face in adoring praise to God, and poured forth such sweet strains of melodious thanksgiving, that David could not withhold his fingers from the strings of his harp. In a moment more, the whole chariot was sounding with the sweetest music of all the ages, for the sweet singer of Israel had greatly improved himself, he said, since he had been singing the songs of heaven. While we were singing, Bohemond arose and joined, and sang so loud and lovely that all eyes were turned upon him. As I scanned the faces I caught the glimpse of one which I soon recognized as that of Abraham whom I had met back at the crystal river. I stepped toward him. He knew me and called my name, and shook my hand with a joyous fresh welcome and said, "Let me introduce to you my son Isaac, and Jacob as well, of whom you have often read."

"Oh, is this your son whom you offered on Mount Moriah? And Jacob, you chosen of God, who wrestled with the angel and prevailed. How blessed to meet you all here! How much like a dream, when we used to read the record of your lives! Oh, my soul is full of glory and praises to God. I am so happy in meeting you here, but you have been here for long ages and I have just come. There are many things I would like to ask you, and I trust in no distant day we may have a long talk. But it does seem good to be here. Just now I remember a Scripture passage which I have read so many times over, but it never had a meaning as it does now. Our Lord once said that: 'Many should come from the East and the West and should sit down with Abraham, Isaac and Jacob in the kingdom of heaven,' (Matthew 8:11), and here it is fulfilled to us. Oh, I do bless God for His great salvation!

"The music sounds so clear and distinct we must be near the great gathering place for the mighty assembly."

"Indeed we are," said David. "Direct your eyes over there and see."

I arose and stood upright in the chariot with one hand on David's shoulder and with the other I held my harp. To my great astonishment, as far as the eye could reach, I saw innumerable crowds gathering and everyone robed in the purest white. The orchestra was still practicing and singing some of the most lovely songs human ears had ever heard. My soul was in a perfect state of rapture and bliss.

The place of the meeting was more like a great amphitheater. The architecture had all been designed by our Lord and is among the things He went to prepare for us. All the seats were beautifully upholstered and the floors carpeted with exquisite taste. Almost without noise or commotion everyone found his place. I said to David, "Will our Lord be here among us?"

"No doubt He is here now," answered David, "and will be seated in the center, and all the fresh arrivals will be ushered to seats near Him. This is done to give them a fresh welcome and that all may see the vast millions of those who are being redeemed and washed by His precious blood, and yet the strangers and newcomers which will be here are only a small portion of those who have so recently entered the portals of paradise, and many of them have entered through the gates into the city."

And true enough, for so it was. All the fresh arrivals were gathered from among the mighty crowd toward the center. Our Lord sat on a kind of elevated throne visible to all the great congregation. He arose and with most loving words gave us a very kind greeting. A deep sense of awe filled our minds. We knew we were standing in the presence of the Almighty Creator and Gracious Redeemer, and we felt great joy in the kind welcome He gave us. He held up His hands, and the nail prints were also seen in His feet. He did not need a sermon to arouse our feelings of praise. Before time could be given for any further introduction we had all fallen on our faces in adoring praise, for we felt so deeply that all this glory was the purchase of His precious blood—His sufferings and death on the cross of Calvary.

In a few moments we all stood on our feet again and received another gracious welcome by our Lord. His words were most tender and loving and the welcome so sweet and full that at once we all felt perfectly at ease and at home with all the rest of the great company and we all praised God together.

Many hundreds of angels were among us who had carried us from the scenes of our earthly lives into the heavenly domain. They seemed to rejoice with great joy that we were safely home in the bosom of God.

Just at this time David arose to his feet and with him many prophets, patriarchs, apostles and ancient servants of God. The song of praise was announced and the whole congregation, having harps of God in their hands, arose. They, or rather we, for we all joined, sang the song of Moses and the song of the Lamb, and the chorus was, "Great and marvelous are Your works, Lord God Almighty. Just and true are Your ways, You King of Saints." (Revelation 15:3) David's harp played that day as I think it had never played on earth.

Paul and Silas stood side by side and their voices could be distinctly heard above the voices of many. Oh, if only the church on earth could catch the inspiration and life of this heavenly worship, there would be few lifeless congregations, even where there is no preacher at all!

When at last the great congregation had broken up and we were scattering in all directions, we met several ancient men and women who had lived far back in the past ages of the world, with some of whom we had very precious visits.

* * *

There were many who remained behind long after the great crowd had dispersed. Many of these were so filled with the glory of God that they seemed to be holding a kind of after service, which I found was always in order. Like it often is on earth during great revival seasons, the Spirit of God is so infused into the people that a congregation is often unwilling to leave the scenes of prayer, and while returning to their homes they would be singing the songs of Zion.

I found that the themes of the highest praise in heaven were often those which had been the greatest blessings of earth. The memories of the past and the conscious sense of great deliverances should always bring the soul a deep sense of its indebtedness and gratitude to God. Among those who remained behind were some ancient men joining with the great choir in many hymns of praise, and singing also many solos of ancient date, of which one could judge by their peculiar wording— referring frequently to events, times, and places of far gone ages—so that we could tell at once that they were ancient men and had lived in a far, remote period of time, although they looked as youthful and full of vigor as any of us who had just entered the city.

To some of these I was especially attracted. Their great earnestness and enthusiasm and distinct behavior, coupled with such lovely faces and sweet tempers, invited us to go and sit among them. So I said to Bohemond, "Let us go and talk with them and find out who they are."

They welcomed us to their company. We soon found ourselves sitting in the presence of Job and Methuselah, Abel and Noah, with many of the earliest ancestors of the race. They all seemed full of vigorous life with no marks of decrepit old age like we knew so much in the world. I then quickly thought of the words of the angel to John: "Behold I make all things new," (Revelation 21:5) and sure enough, these were among the earliest of the race of man, made in God's image, on whom this mighty rejuvenating power had come.

We had a long but very pleasant visit with them asking them many questions concerning the early history of man on the earth.

Adam and Eve were the first creation of man in the image of God.

We arose to bid them good-bye, when they embraced us with an affectionate kiss and said, "We'll see you again."

Bohemond and myself now went to a quiet place and sat down to talk over the things we had just heard and witnessed for we were most deeply impressed with the words of these ancient men. "Oh," I said, "what is the full and utmost meaning of eternal life? If four thousand years have not made their mark of feebleness, nor dimmed the eye, nor cooled the love and zeal of these men, surely eternity never will."

There were many coming and going, and everyone had such a sweet and holy attitude and disposition with such pleasant smiles of loveliness that revealed eternal satisfaction and contentment. I said to Bohemond, "I have been thinking about a number of my old friends and relatives in the earth who, if they only knew what we know now, they would lead very different lives and seek to be ready for this solid glory."

Bohemond replied, "I almost wish, myself, I could return for just a few days and tell my own people, to whom religion is but little more than an empty profession, the great realities of this heavenly kingdom. I myself never thought it was half so real or could be so grand."

"Well, Bohemond, I would be glad to have you tell me something of your earthly life and surroundings."

"I am descended," said Bohemond, "from a race of kings of Norman blood who reigned for many years at Antioch in Syria. After the close of the dynasty, which occurred about the close of the thirteenth century, our family scattered to different countries, but principally to Bohemia. Our people soon joined in with the Bohemian brethren, many of them becoming earnest followers of Christ. A great persecution arose and many were compelled to hide themselves in dens and caves of the earth. But with the exodus of about a thousand brethren to Poland in the last of the fifteenth century, the honorable sires of our family came.

"By the principles of our faith we were forbidden all kinds of warfare as not fitting with the teaching of our Lord. Because of this and the denial of the doctrine of transubstantiation, persecution was still heaped upon us. Later on, our particular family moved to northern Russia where we have been ever since. Many of them have grown wealthy and very prosperous, but I am sad to know that many among them have substituted wealth on earth for treasures in heaven.[2] If they only knew what was reserved in store for all the redeemed and blood-washed, which we are now enjoying, and were it real to them as it is to us I feel sure they would mightily bestir themselves. Oh, could I send them one warning message from heaven, they would hear me, would they not?"

"Well," I replied, "Abraham was of a different opinion. They have Moses and the prophets; if they would not hear them neither would they hear if one should rise from the dead, so why should we want to return?" We sat long, talking these matters over, but when we finally looked around we found that the great congregation had nearly all gone. But David's chariot still remained standing near the entrance where the crowds had gathered. I said to Bohemond, "Listen a moment. Isn't that lovely music? And the song, oh, how soul-stirring it is." We looked through the great archway toward the chariot and saw David motioning us to him. We hurried through the long aisle and when near the chariot, we found it was filled with those holy men of old.

David now said, "We saw you were quite alone and thought you would like to go with us to a great praise service for the children soon to be held near the Judean gate."

We gladly accepted their offer, saying, "We were on our way to the Throne, but will be glad to go with you for we are not very well acquainted with the city."

Paul spoke lovingly, and yet laughingly, and said, "Well, dear brethren, I have been here for more than eighteen hundred years and yet I know but little of the city, although I have been to many sections of it again and again. Our inheritance is exceedingly great. Don't hurry—eternity is before you. The vast plains of paradise," said Paul, "and all the riches of the eternal city are yours forever."

---

2. This incident obviously had taken place before Communism took over in Russia in 1917. -Engeltal Press (EP)

A Great Prayer Meeting in Heaven

"Now," said David, "step up and take a seat beside Paul and myself. Those brethren in the rear of the chariot would be glad to speak to you." The four men arose, and we were introduced to Elijah and Daniel, whom everyone knows, and who are famous in heaven on account of their devotion and service to God in the earth, and a man by the name of Artorious, of whom I had never heard before. David said he was from Southern Mesopotamia and a descendant from Shem and one of Abraham's soldiers in the battle at Hobah in the King's Dale, and John the beloved disciple, whose name is a household word in all the world.

"Well, brethren," I said, "is it true that we are here with those who have lived so long ago? The idea of immortality and a future life, which we cherished so dearly in the world has proven more than a dream. Oh, how good it is to be here! There are so many things I want to ask you concerning a far bygone age, but my soul is too full of glory and praises to God now, I cannot restrain my feelings."

David said, "You don't need to try. We will all join you in praises to God." Silas arose from the front of the chariot and came and stood by David's side while they sang a most lovely hymn. Bohemond and I fell on our faces in the chariot and worshipped God, blessed Giver of all this good.

*   *   *

David led in the singing of the hymn. The chariot was moving slowly along. When we finished David said to his charioteer, "You may drive past the children's Polytechnic, and let our brethren so recently come see what our Lord has prepared for the little ones of His kingdom." So, turning to the right, he guided the chariot, not too quickly, for we had many things to talk about on the way.

The avenue was broad and lovely. We passed many gushing fountains and groves of the trees of life. These were not for shade as no burning sun strikes either the city or the blessed paradise.

On the way I said to Paul, who sat by my side, "It does seem so good to be here with you; it seems indeed too good to be true. Fancy painted many wonderful pictures while we were in the world which were made to glow on the canvas of our imagination in reference to the future, but none ever equaled the reality."

"No," said Paul, "it was impossible for man to conceive of the glory while in the flesh. The Lord once gave me just a glimpse into paradise while yet in the world. The glory was beyond my power to describe."

I replied to Paul, "I have often wondered how it occurred, for we have a brief account in the divine word on earth which you left concerning it. (2 Corinthians 12:2-4)

"Well," said he, "while at Lystra in Lyconia I was stoned and dragged out of the city for dead, but God raised me up, and I, with the brethren, went back to the city." (Acts 14:19) "But that night I could not sleep, being restless and burdened with the word of the Lord. I arose and, all alone, went out of the city to pray. I ascended the side of old Karadogh, an extinct volcano. I seemed to be greatly helped, for an angel constantly held my hand. When some little distance up the mountain, one of the chariots of God, with a driver of light, appeared at my side. I was so enraptured by the presence and glory of God and both over-awed and overcome by the royal chariot and driver that I hardly could tell whether I had died or was in a trance, but I soon found myself lying prostrate in the chariot and ascending far above the old mountain. We arose above the pillars of the skies. I soon heard the strains of music from the third heaven in the plains of paradise. They were singing some new songs, which as a mortal man, I had no power to repeat. I opened my eyes just for a moment, glanced at the crystal river and heard a loud voice proclaiming the mystery of the trees upon its banks. It was the closing words of a sermon uttered by Moses to a vast company of Jews, as I was told by the driver afterwards, shining light upon these things that they could not know while under the law and subject to an inferior experience—for you have already found that we have preaching here in heaven as we used to have on earth.

"Only an instant we remained and the chariot darted with the speed of sound toward the earth. In a few moments the old town of Lystra, lying at the foot of the mountain, with its streets and domes, shone out with their best appearance under the light of the full moon beaming upon them, but the people were fast asleep. I stepped from the chariot as the driver, with a pleasant wave of his hand, said, good-bye, and in an instant it was gone. On the top of Karadogh I continued my prayer and praise to God until near the break of day. I never could really tell while in my flesh whether I was loosened for the time being from my body or whether bodily I was taken to glory. Ever after this I had a strong desire to go back and stay forever—to depart and be with Christ. The words of the sermon and the strains of music could never be forgotten, but were an element of strength in my life during the many afflictions God permitted to come upon me.

"I remember the words in your Epistle," I replied, "'For me to live is Christ and to die is gain. For I am in a strait betwixt two having a desire to depart and be with Christ which is far better.'" (Philippians 1:21)

"Indeed," said Paul, "and had I known all the bliss and glory of the celestial kingdom, as it is, I could not have been contented. I was greatly favored of God, and through so many revelations of His will and manifestations of His power I was in great danger of being unduly exalted, but God always knows how to deal with us for our greatest good. A man of most bitter wrath was turned against me, indeed he was a thorn in the flesh to me. He was the messenger of Satan, but God's grace then, as at all times, was entirely sufficient for me, and I always found that all things work together for good to them who love God."

"Oh, thank you much for your words. It seems as if God directed you to give me this little bit of your experience. I have often wondered what the thorn was to which you alluded in the Epistle."

"Yes," said Paul, "but this messenger of Satan, as well as the prisons, scourges, beatings, betrayals by false brethren, and sufferings of earth, only worked for my good. I am so blessedly free from them all now. The contrast is so great it gives me an eternal appreciation of the blessedness of this kingdom."

"I see," said David, "we are coming near the children's spiritual Polytechnic. Can you hear them singing?"

"Oh, most distinctly," and yet, the place was still out of

sight. The streets were crowded with the little ones, usually in company with the angels or faithful mothers or those having care over them. They all seemed so joyous and their laugh of hilarity and joyful conversation revealed their perfect contentment and satisfaction, and yet we knew that most of them had left their parents in the earth, but there is no grief nor sorrow in heaven. If all mothers on earth could only see their children whom they have lost, as they really are, they would weep no more, but make every provision needed to soon follow them to those mansions of light.

Many older people were among them. Some were parents looking after their own children. Some small infants were carried by the angels, or precious women had them pressed close to their bosoms, for their infant feet had never learned to walk.

At last our chariot stopped just near the great entrance, where it seemed countless crowds were pouring in, and of all this great multitude none had been within the reaches of the heavenly domain for very long. Children soon grow to maturity in heaven. Your little babe, dear mother of earth, which left you many years ago, is now with its harp of gold singing and praising God in all the maturity of its manhood or womanhood.

We now stepped out and followed the great crowd wherever they went.

CHAPTER SIX
The Children's Great Cathedral

The place was most beautiful indeed. The decorations were beyond description, for everyone seemed to take an interest in the children and had brought flowers celestial, worked into bouquets and wreaths of artistic beauty, with blooming shrubbery of an unfading character and of many kinds. I thought of the Scripture: "Strength and beauty are in His sanctuary." (Psalm 96:6) "Beautiful and grand indeed!" I whispered. The decorations overhead, the carpets underfoot, the upholstery and cushions were of the finest fabric, with tiny seats also of celestial velvet, for the little ones. A thousand golden chains sparkling with diamonds, and gems of rarest beauty were arranged for the leaders in the service. A large and beautifully arranged platform was in the center on which several thousand could sit or stand, elevated so that all could easily be seen and heard. This was for the leaders in the great public services.

Great multitudes of children were quickly filing in, and gathering towards this great center. They had escorts guiding them to their respective places. They, like all the inhabitants of heaven, were clothed in shining garments of the purest white. They had all entered the portals of the heavenly domain at some point of paradise, for it will be remembered that all souls enter paradise first of all, and as they are prepared for the fuller enjoyment of the King and His glory, they pass on toward the

Throne where God Himself is seen and enjoyed in all His glory and majesty.

All these children had been for a longer or shorter period in the preparatory departments of paradise, but they had now entered through the gates with greatly extended privileges.

As I glanced over the countless multitude of little ones, I was most strongly reminded of the words of our Lord: "Suffer the children to come unto me, and forbid them not, for of such is the kingdom of heaven." (Mark 10:14) I thought again that no longer was the warning needed that: "Whosoever shall offend one of these little ones which believe in me, it were better for him that a millstone were hanged about his neck and that he were drowned in the depths of the sea." (Mark 9:42) 'No,' I thought, 'thank God, no more experiences of being cuffed about as many had been on earth. No more little heartaches and sobs. No more being falsely accused and blamed by irritated older ones!'

I thought as I looked over this wonderful gathering that every child had a history of its own. I thought of little Mary and her sad story of whom we used to sing on earth. A mother who was preparing some flour for baking into cakes left it for a few minutes when little Mary, with childish curiosity to see what it was, took hold of the dish which fell to the floor spilling the contents. The mother struck the child a severe blow, saying, with anger, that she was always in the way. A fortnight afterward little Mary's sickness had increased to her death. On her death bed while delirious she asked her mother if there would be any room for her among the angels. "I was always in your way, mother, you had no room for me at times in your heart. And shall I be in the angels' way?" The broken-hearted mother then felt no sacrifice too great, could she have saved the child.

When the dewy light was fading
And the sky in beauty smiled,
Came this whisper, like an echo,
From a pale and dying child:

The Children's Great Cathedral

"Mother, in that golden region
With its pearly gates so fair,
Up among the happy angels,
Is there room for Mary there?

"Mother, raise me just a moment;
You'll forgive me when I say
You were angry when you told me
I was always in your way.

"You were sorry in a moment,
I could read it on your brow,
But you'll not recall it, mother;
You must never mind it now.

"When my baby sister calls me
And you hear my voice no more;
When she plays among the roses
By our little cottage door;

"Never chide her when you're angry.
Do it kindly and in love:
That you both may dwell with Mary,
In the sunny land above."

Then she plumed her snowy pinions
Till she folded them to rest.
Mid the welcome song of rapture
On the loving Saviour's breast.

In the bright and golden regions,
With its pearly gates so fair,
She is singing with the angels.
Yes, there's room for Mary there.

I wondered and said to myself, 'Is she among these countless crowds I see?' Everyone seemed to be so contented and happy and without that feeling of loneliness and fear which is so natural to all children on earth when absent from parents or home. They seemed to be so rational and appreciative of their situation. Some of them had died when tiny infants and had known nothing of the earth, so they seemed to be somewhat amused at the story of their former life and beginning in the world. "Oh, this wonderful scene: the grandest I have ever witnessed either on earth or in heaven," I said to Bohemond. "My whole soul is in raptures of delight." We could hear the voices of thousands who were praising God, with loud, yet most sweet words, and with their harps of gold. The great amphitheater was simply ringing with the melodies of heaven. David's chariot stood still on the street, but he with the remainder of our company had gone on toward the great central gathering, for our Lord Himself was seated on the platform, blessing the multitude as they came past. His blessing was filled with such enlightening grace that the children suddenly broke out with such intelligent praise that one might think they had been here for many years.

Just at this moment I was very happy to see dear mother coming toward me. I had parted from her at my first introduction to Moses when she went outside the gate to assist a group of these little ones.

"Oh, mother," I shouted, "I am so glad to meet you again. Have you been with these children ever since you left me when we were talking with Moses, for you went to take charge of a group of children singing their songs just outside the gate?"

"Yes, indeed, and they are now among this mighty crowd praising God and for the first time they look upon their Saviour's face and receive His gracious welcome."

* * *

"I should like to know who this is with you, mother, who seems to bear the family likeness." I noticed an eager smile upon the face of a beautiful young woman who stood beside her.

"Well," said my mother, "I have been waiting to see if you would recognize her, for you once knew her as a little infant"

"Oh, mother, I want to know if this is my own darling child who left us when only three months from her birth!"

"Indeed," replied mother, "this is your child and I have watched over her ever since she came into paradise."

From that moment she hugged me with deep and sweet praises to God. We could not weep, for there are no tears in heaven, but our rejoicing was more precious than anything I had ever known on earth. "Well," I said, "dear child, I only knew you as a little infant, but now you have grown to womanhood. We wept much when you died, for our home was deserted and stripped of all the light and joy which you brought into it. Your mother and I were not active Christians then, but for many days and nights we could hear your voice with a plaintive cry calling us to this city of light."

"Oh," said Mary, for that was her name, "it was the angel who carried me to paradise, for he went back to speak to you for your cheer and comfort, so he told me later on."

"Well, my dear child, I am so glad to see you once again after more than forty years have passed, now grown to your maturity. How graceful you look! You must have been well cared for."

"Cared for! No soul lacks attention in heaven. This your mother has been my mother since my tiny life in paradise began. But I have often met my real mother, for she was here long before you came. Have you not met her yet?"

"No, dear child, but I know I will soon. I have asked after her quite often, but I find she is detained in some distant place in paradise assisting a group of young people who had recently come, but who were not prepared for the glory of the city, and she cannot leave them just now."

"Yes," said Mary, "I know quite well where she is and have been to see her often."

"Among many others whose bodies were buried beside your own, we lost your little grave, but we knew you were not lost. The meeting which we had looked forward to seemed so like a dream, but, oh, how real it is! Your mother no doubt has told you all about our family which you never knew, but when we have an opportunity we will talk it all over."

"Oh, indeed, I will be delighted to hear you tell me all about each one of them—no, I mean, each one of us."

"Well, dear mother, I am glad you have brought my child to

me. But will you tell me something about the law of growth and development in heaven from that of a tiny infant to the maturity and development which I see before me?"

"Well, you know that the trees of life have twelve kinds of fruit, adapted to all the needs of the human soul. There is no lack of opportunity, for the means of knowledge and instruction are abundantly offered here, according to the growing demands of each soul. Yet the growth and development of each depends much upon its own efforts. There are but few idle people in heaven and yet traits of character developed on earth during the formative period of life continue with us here unless they are changed or overcome during the probationary state. Everyone has his identity and peculiar characteristics developed during his life. If an individual was slack and lazy in his earthly life, the same tendencies continue with him here. There is, however, no such thing as a stubborn or obstinate spirit among all these children, nor in all heaven. Every will bows in sweet harmony with God, but some make more rapid advancement than others, which depends upon their own exertions and energy. As they apply themselves to all the means of instruction and partake wisely of the fruit of the trees, they move along the lines of heavenly development. A similar law prevails here as on earth. Natural law indeed is extended into the spiritual realm. Our souls never cease to grow and develop intellectually and expand their grasp of eternal realities. There is a grand perfection in heaven which allows for an eternal progress toward the fullness of our great Father in whose image we all are. But as on earth, so in the kingdom of heaven, much of our duty and labor of love is for each other, and ever will be."

I then said to my mother, "Persons who have been separated but a short time will see and know each other much as they saw them when they parted in the world."

"Quite the same," she said, "only the difference between the earthly and the heavenly state. But in the case of parents whose little ones were taken in infancy and the parents remained in the world for many years, they shall not meet them as infants, but like yours, developed toward maturity."

"Oh, yes, I see, it would be a great calamity if they should remain tiny infants or were untaught little children."

"Now, look over this great company," said mother. "You see multitudes of classes formed and the angels, elders, and more experienced ones are teaching them the knowledge of heaven and new hymns of praise, and soon we will all join in some choruses and if you have never heard music, you will hear it now, when all these children are praising God together, for most of them have learned to use their harps."

Mary, who had been standing nearby listening to our conversation, came up close and said, "I am so glad, dear father, to see you here. How long since you have come?"

"Only a short time," I replied.

"I hope soon to hear all about our family since mother left you and even before, for you may tell me some things she has not. I do not know why I was taken from you so early, but our good Father knows best and all He does is best and just at the right time. I remember being a little infant in your arms and on mother's breast, but I haven't much recollection of the world, but I am told it is much inferior to this land of light and joy."

Her memory was doing its work. She took me by the hand and hugged once more and began to praise God in such sweet tones that it seemed for the time that all the events for nearly forty years were annihilated and we stood as father and infant.

Just at this moment my companions of the chariot, who had gone on toward the center of the great hall, motioned to me. We all went toward them and at a given signal the mighty assembly fell upon their faces in adoring praise to Him who was in the midst and was fairer than the sons of men. Many of these children looked upon His blessed face for the first time. Such a welcome He gave them, which showed His great love for the little ones.

The harps were all tuned to the voice of the singer, and as we now arose, all stood, and many with outstretched hands toward Him with one great voice made the arches and domes of heaven to resound with melodious infant praises. How strongly I again remembered the words: "Suffer the little children to come unto me for of such is the kingdom of heaven." (Mark 10:14)

These meetings I found were frequently for the children

83

in which they were taught the worship of God and instructed concerning the sad fact of sin, and that without the great atoning sacrifice of their Lord, none of them could ever have entered the blessed portals of this heavenly domain. They were taught about His sufferings and death for them, the sin and awful fall of our first parents in Eden, and how judgment came upon all to condemnation, and that an eternal night of hell would have been theirs if their Lord had not suffered for them. I noticed their intense interest in the story of the cross and their deep appreciation of what the Lord had done for them. The prints of the nails yet in His hands and feet were an object lesson to them indeed.

The time came at last for dismissal. The great assembly arose, and the doxology began:

> Praise God, Great Author of all love,
> Praise Him all creatures here above,
> Praise Him below, a mighty host:
> Praise Father, Son, and Holy Ghost.[3]

As we sang the doxology, it seemed that earth and heaven had united. The veil between seemed very thin. In fact, we knew we were all one great family and that very soon all of earth's redeemed would be forever together. The benediction was pronounced by our Lord Himself, with such blessed words of heavenly love, it seemed like He might almost be back upon earth blessing the little children.

We were soon scattering in all directions, but the children's joyous songs and faces beaming with such expression of contentment, as they were passing through the great archway, constantly attracted my attention.

I said, "What perfect satisfaction, so complete is their joy! They have all the company anyone could wish. No one longs for company not found here. There is no danger, nor any feeling of fear. There is no one in all the wide domain of this heavenly

---

3. In heaven the wording of doxology is changed to fit the place where it is sung. -EP

kingdom with any evil intent or desire, but perfect confidence and trust in every soul."

David who came near me just then with his harp strings trembling with an air of peculiar sweetness and who seemed to be enjoying the grand procession as well, stopped nearby. I said to him, "Do you find any homesick children wanting to go back to their old homes in the earth?"

"Not one," he replied. "If parents could only see and know this glory into which their children have entered they would not mourn over their departure from the earth so bitterly."

I said to David, "I remember just now your word concerning your own child when it had died. Your grief had been most intolerable during its sickness, but when it was dead, you said, 'I shall go to him, but he shall not return to me.'" (2 Samuel 12:23)

"Yes," said David, "and I have been with him nearly three thousand years in this glory. Twenty years after his death I followed him and found he had grown to mature years and had been a thousand times in similar places as this and much instructed in the ways of the eternal city." [g]

*   *   *

As we were leaving the children's great convocation, David came and asked if we would like to take a quick trip into paradise. As his chariot was now going, we gladly accepted the invitation, and in a short time mother, myself and my daughter stepped out of the chariot about six thousand kilometers[4] from the gate of Manasseh. This was a new but most beautiful place in paradise to us. David said, "Enjoy yourselves as you like. I will call for you later," and his chariot moved on. In the distance I saw another chariot reducing its speed. Four souls clothed in the garments of heaven were seated inside. To one of them I was particularly drawn. He was clothed in a white gown only. The moment he found he was within the gates of paradise and opening his eyes upon the glory before him, he fell prostrate upon his face with the deepest emotion, both of praise and

---

4. "A thousand leagues." That is about 3,500 miles. A league being about 5.7 kilometres (3.5 miles).

regrets over the past. He was greatly bewildered over the glory of which he felt so unworthy. He tried to praise God but could not look up for shame, he was so nearly naked.

One of the saints who seemed to understand his situation addressed him and said, "You are saved. Think not of your past. What God has forgiven He remembers no more."

"Yes," said the man, "but I am so unworthy. The angels assured me that the gate would be open for me. Only a few hours ago I was a lost sinner and far from God. I have come direct from the jaws of eternal death. Oh, tell me, am I in heaven? The sermon I cannot forget. Oh, how God blessed the preacher! His words went to my heart. I was grieving over my sins and crying. I was praying—Oh, how Jesus revealed Himself to me, and gave me rest! I was on my dying bed. They called for a meeting and our house was crowded, only last night. Oh, tell me, I pray you, am I in heaven?"

"You are safe," the saint replied, "safe at home. Can you repeat any of the sermon to us?"

"Indeed I can, every word of it. Hosea 10:12. 'Is it time to seek the Lord? At 5 a.m. when the first gleams of the morning appear, you ask, "Is it time to seek the Lord?" A voice from heaven whispers, "They that seek Me early shall find Me." At 7 a.m. again you ask, "Is it now time to seek the Lord?" A voice from the Throne replies, "Remember now your Creator in the days of your youth." Oh, what a beautiful Light is circling round the brow and becoming a center of joy within the character of that child of God who has early learned to lisp the name of Jesus! Again at 9 a.m. the bell calls and you ask, "Is it time to seek the Lord?" Conscience trembles and says, "I have passed many an open door of grace already and the sins of my youth are multiplied." As you listen to the voice you hear it saying, "Now is the accepted time: now is the day of salvation." High noon has now come to many a soul here. The most important period of life has already past or is now upon you. The golden opportunities of childhood and youth will return to you no more. Yet you say with an indifferent air, "Is it time for me to seek the Lord?" Satan now begins to whisper, "Your heart is hard, you cannot easily repent with all your cares upon you."

"'Turn your eyes upward and listen,' the preacher said. 'As you say, "What must I do to be saved?" everything within you has been saying, "Repent, repent." Now the echo comes back from heaven as though sounded with the trump of God, "Repent ye and believe the gospel. Come unto me and I will give you rest. In the day that ye seek me with all the heart I will be found of you."

"'Consider your situation as it is in God's sight. Think you of the littleness of time that is left you for so great a preparation. Think you of your accountability to God. You will soon stand before Him, and render an impartial account of your stewardship. Think you of your reply to Him who sits upon the Throne when He shall say, "Friend, how have you come in here not having on a wedding garment?" (Matthew 22:12) Oh, think of your feelings when you will look this way and that, to find yourself so confounded that you are speechless, as you recall the days when showers of grace from heaven fell so often upon you, and your heart yielded no fruit of righteousness in return. Think of the barren fig tree that stood so many years in the vineyard, having been dug about and watered so long without any fruit, that when mercy shall cry, "Cut it down," anticipate your sorrow and think what your feelings will be.

"'Think deeply of the weeds which have been growing in your heart so long and scattering their seed in other soil around you. Think of the ripening harvest from your sowing, and that, "Whatsoever a man sows, that shall he also reap." Think of the rich man in torment, remembering good only to lighten his sorrow, knowing it might have been otherwise with his soul, but now being tormented he could see "Lazarus afar off in Abraham's bosom."

"'As these considerations are before you, hurry with all speed to Him who alone is able to save you. Oh, do not live longer as if there were neither a bed of death nor a bar of judgment. Be wise. Look your danger in the face. Anticipate the day when you shall behold a God in judgment and a world in flames, and flee to your God from the wrath to come.'"

With this the man bowed his head again and with sobs of emotion mingled with joy and grief, he arose and said, "Oh, thank God, I remember it all and was earnestly praying when the chariot called for me. Oh, I did and do hate every sin of the past. I do love God. I am His forever. Hallelujah to Jesus!"

Quite a group had gathered to hear this sermon. When he had finished we all united in one great shout of praise to God.

"Oh, yes," he said, "I am in heaven! Thank God for His everlasting mercy. I am out of hell. I am in heaven."

When he had finished his sermon my mother and daughter went to him and said, "Good brother, we rejoice with you that you are in heaven. You see your folly in not having made better preparation for this land of light and love, but be faithful to every opportunity for your advancement. Your guides will instruct you into the ways and laws of this heavenly kingdom."

I also gave him words of cheer, and he began to praise God again and said, "I do bless God for that preacher. His words were surely sent by the Holy Spirit. They went like an arrow to my soul."

At this an elder came and said to him, "Be of good cheer, my brother, the angels have brought you safely to this paradise and far toward the interior from the gate of entrance. Many of the ancient saints spend much time about the threshold of paradise and assist all who enter. But a large number of them have just been up to some great praise services within the city and have not yet returned, and the angel has brought you here. Pay good heed to all your opportunities, for much is before you."

"Oh," he cried out, "only let me know what I must do to be in harmony with this holy place. Oh, heaven, you are mine! Am I at all purified from my sin? Oh, am I acceptable to God. Will He welcome me?"

"Surely," said the elder, "when you are prepared for the light and glory of the city, you will be brought to its gates and ushered in with the welcome of your Lord. If you wait among these trees, do not be restless nor neglectful. Almost the entire catalogue of the Christian graces must be learned by you. Partake freely of the twelve kinds of fruit on the trees, they will impart light, life and grace to your soul. Press the leaves to your nostrils and bind them to your heart and no taint of evil will remain in you."

At this we saw David's chariot coming in the distance.

CHAPTER SEVEN
An Excursion with the Martyred Saints

avid's chariot was now here. With him were a number of new arrivals but who were full fledged saints of earth. With exultant praises they were glorifying God. Their faces beaming with the light of heaven. David called to us, saying, "I'll see you again later. Go where you will. I must take these dear brethren far up the river toward the gate of Manasseh, where they will spend some time among the trees which you can see in the far distance over there." As the chariot moved off, David's harp strings were trembling to the words of the twenty-fourth Psalm, in which all had joined.

My mother now said, "Over there comes four beautiful spirits whom I want you to meet. They are the most joyful souls I have met in a long time. I have often met them in the city and know them quite well."

As they came nearer I asked her who they were.

"They were of the martyred saints," she replied. "They were all burnt at the stake, for their testimony for our Lord."

"Oh, mother, I shall be so glad to meet them."

"And I too," said Mary.

By this time they were very near us. A wonderful halo of glory was about them.

"Good morning," said mother, for everyone says good morning in heaven for a long time after they have entered paradise or even the city gates, for it seems as though morning had only come, one feels so refreshed, happy and light-hearted. They returned the greeting with a lovely bow and handshake. We were soon introduced and a lively conversation following and indeed it was a joyful meeting. Their holy, heavenly laugh and joyful expressions filled my soul with rapture of praise.

"My mother has just told me that you are of those who once suffered martyrdom for Christ's sake."

"Yes," said one of them, "we remember those days of awful persecution as though it were but yesterday. But many hundreds of years have passed since then and we are amply repaid for it here. They tried hard to force us to renounce, but no, our Lord's words were too close to our hearts for that. He had said, 'Fear not them which kill the body but are not able to kill the soul, but rather fear him which is able to destroy both soul and body in hell.' (Matthew 10:28) Our sufferings were intense, but it was soon over and we were immediately ushered into this glory. As we leaped from the body we shouted victory over fire and enemies."

As they uttered these words I thought of the Scripture where John, the beloved disciple, said: "I saw under the altar the souls of them that were slain for the word of God and for the testimony which they held. And they cried with a loud voice, saying, 'How long, O Lord, holy and true, do you not judge and avenge our blood on them that dwell on the earth?' And white robes were given to every one of them, and it was said unto them that they should rest yet for a little season until their fellow servants also and their brethren should be killed as they were." (Revelation 6:10-11)

"Indeed," said they all, "and our rest has been most sweet among these bowers of paradise and the glories of the eternal city."

"It is here," said one of them, "as it used to be on earth when the old soldiers of war times would have their reunions and festivities, and talk over the memories of their awful struggles. We are just now headed for a great reunion of the martyrs and confessors of our Lord during the dark ages of bitter persecution on earth. In a little while you will see many chariots bringing their thousands to what we call here, 'Our excursion to the hills.' We would be pleased to have you go along with us."

Mary quickly spoke up and said, "Yes, let us go."

We quickly dropped in with them and walked to the station just near. While waiting for a chariot I said to mother and Mary, "I am so glad for this meeting. I have heard so much of the days of awful persecution and of the thousands who were killed by fire and sword. Nero's persecution at Rome was an awful time when he burnt so many of the saints. Smearing their nude bodies with pitch and making midnight torches of them, and their agonizing cries were the music for his chariot races."

"It was terrible," said mother, "but they are all here now with the glory of God upon them. No doubt we will meet many of them soon."

"Look," said Mary, "do you see the chariots coming?"

"Oh, yes, in the distance," I replied. "Is their route past this station?"

"I think so," said one of the saints, and with that he waved the flowing ends of his mantle and a charioteer seeing him turned his chariot toward us. As it came near, I noticed there were a number of coaches attached somewhat like our railroad train cars on earth. I did not yet know the propelling power of the chariots, but something like the electrical currents of earth strongly operated these wonderful fliers of heaven. [h]

As the chariot slowed its speed and drew near us, we all stepped aboard and were greeted by hundreds of the most joyful people I have met in heaven. The chariot moved on with wonderful speed toward the pleasure parks and hillsides of paradise. When at last it slowed down amid a mighty crowd gathering from all parts of the city of those who had been beheaded and martyred for Christ's sake. Many of them had suffered untold anguish and tortures in prisons, at racks and inquisitions, torn of wild beasts in the arena of amphitheaters for the amusement of wicked men. We saw many of those alluded to in the blessed Book which now lies on your table, where it speaks of Gideon and Barak and Samson and Jephthah and David and Samuel and the prophets and others which had trials of cruel mockings and scourgings, or bonds and imprisonments. We saw those who had been stoned, sawn asunder, were tempted, were slain with the sword, who had wandered about in sheepskins and goatskins, being destitute, afflicted, tormented: Of whom the world was not worthy. They had wandered in deserts and in mountains and dens and caves of the earth.

Among them we saw James whom Herod killed with the sword, and Stephen whom they stoned—in fact, nearly all the apostles were there. We saw also Latimer and Thomas Hawks and a hundred beside who had suffered in England as martyrs under the reign of her who was called "Bloody Mary." But they with the thousands of others who had sealed their testimony with their own blood, were the most joyful of all men whom I had met in all the heavenly domain. During the course of the exercises of the occasion and the joyful and exultant praises from this great army of saints over whom neither fire, sword, nor prison could prevail to make them deny their holy confession of Jesus, I kept thinking of that Scripture where in the Revelation of St. John he says: "I saw the souls of them who were beheaded for the witness of Jesus and for the word of God, and which had not worshipped the beast neither his image, neither had received his mark upon their foreheads, nor in their hands, and they lived and reigned with Christ a thousand years." (Revelation 20:4)

Just at this time Paul came to us and seeing I was but a newcomer to this great feast, said to me, "Were you a martyr for Jesus?"

I said, "No, but I truly love Him and hope I am not intruding."

"Oh, no," he replied, "you are indeed welcome."

I was then emboldened to ask him to explain that Scripture just quoted.

"Certainly," said he, "all this great number who have suffered for Christ on earth shall also likewise reign with Him on earth. The millennial Sabbath is almost to dawn, when for a thousand years these will be greatly honored among the hosts of heaven when the Lord shall return to earth with all His saints. They shall reign with Him. This honor have all the martyred saints, for they who suffer with Him shall also reign with Him."

When the great assembly had closed its business session (for there is much business carried on in heaven of which the business in the earth is but child's play in comparison), then followed the praise service which for enthusiasm and spiritual activity would put to blush most of our active services in the church on earth. The harps and stringed instruments of heaven, in the hands of these trained choir singers, simply made the arches and domes of heaven ring. Souls developed under such trials of suffering as these had passed through, who make up this mighty convocation, brought forth the sweetest and loveliest melodies, until I was simply bewildered in the consideration of the capacity and development of a human soul in heaven.

Following this was a heavenly picnic, which for joy and gladness and demonstration of victories and praise, nothing in earth will compare to it. Fruits of many kinds with the various spices and provisions of the eternal world were prepared for the lunch. Angels were busy at this service. It was difficult for me to learn of the multitudes of good things prepared for these saints, there was such an abundance. After all had eaten, then the thousands began their rambles through the valleys and among the hills and mountains of paradise. Great gorges with stupendous cataracts and magnificent scenery and pleasant places of rest and enjoyment abounded everywhere. Perpetual blooming flowers with groves of trees and carpets of grass with such endless varieties bring their constant rewards to those who rest from their labors, with an eternal satisfaction in this blessed paradise above.

* * *

At the close of the great convocation, mother came to me and said, "Son, have you noticed there is no race prejudice in heaven?"

"No distinctions of the races, mother?"

"Yes, there are distinctions, but no prejudice because of race. It makes no difference here as to the kind of body we had on earth. All souls have a spotless whiteness here and their robes, the same. Whatever the physical condition may have been on earth, we are all one family here. Children of one Father. Do you notice that group of singers over there?"

"I do, mother."

"They were all colored people of America," she said. "Some of them suffered much, as slaves, by their old masters. Let us go and speak to them a moment."

We did so, when to my great surprise I quickly recognized one of them. We stood face to face, but for a moment I hesitated, and then said, "In the name of paradise, is this you, Rastus?"

"Oh," he said, "it's me, but who be you?"

I said, "Look again."

He did so and began to smile. "I do know you, Mr. Sodi. You preached to us colored folks once on board the vessel on de North Sea," and with that he gave me his hand.

I knew him in my earlier years having business with his old master in the South. He was very dark-skinned and uneducated, but his face now shone with the brightness of heaven itself, and his garments were perfect whiteness.

"Well, I am glad to meet you," he said.

"Indeed, it is mutual," I replied. "But you are so changed. Are there no black faces in heaven?" I inquired.

"Oh," he said, "we are all white here and in de perfect image of de Lord."

I asked what his old master thought of the great exaltation into which he had come.

"My master," said he, "I fear is not here. I have never seen him since I escaped him and went to northern Russia on de vessel of which you know. De floggin' had been a hard one and I determined he'd never give me anoder one. So after de vessel was full of de cotton bales I hid underneath 'em till she was well out at sea, when I made myself known because of hunger and thirst. They made many threats to throw me over into the sea, like to Jonah, but my life was spared and I escaped to Russia. Neither have I seen him in dis heavenly world. I have passed to and fro among these countless hosts of de redeemed and have been to very many sections of de city, but I have not met him. I fear he is not here. He used to attend de services of his church and made a good profession on de Sunday, but during de week he was ungodly and rough to his children and still worse to us his slaves. I have been made to feel so deeply de folly of servin' de Lord one day in de seven and de devil de udder six. Thousands are lost tryin' to serve two masters and 'peerin' to be good on de Sunday and let de devil rule 'em de rest of de week. Oh, I was so poor in de world—my cabin had no window, nor did we have a rag of a carpet on de floor, nor a picture on de wall, neither did we have a flower in de yard nor did we have a yard, for the cotton growed to de door.

"But oh, I have everything here; everything I kin see is mine. And all beside and still it belongs to all dese udder people just as much as me. I goes just where I like, up and down de streets, through de long avenues, out through de gates of de city in de blessed chariots of God, to de infinite regions of dis paradise, and de Lord Jesus has given me entire liberty and says, 'Go jis whar you will, and eat of every tree you like. Clime de mountains and go into de valley and along de rivers and bathe your soul in de sunshine of de Lamb, who is de light of all de heavenly city and dis paradise.'"

"Well, Rastus," I said to him, "I am very glad to meet you here and witness how God has lifted you up from the dust and the dung hill and made you a prince among His saints."

"Indeed, I am gladder dan you kin be. I am de object of His grace and you de witness. But when did you come to de city?"

"This," I replied, "is my first visit to paradise after having been in the city only a short time. I have only just begun to see my inheritance."

"Well," said he, "you will never git tired lookin' into de great mysteries of de eternal city. Nor will your heart ever shrivel again under de cold blasts of de world of sin, but it will swell wid de highest emotions of praise. Do you see dis harp (which he loosened from his belt and began to test the strings)? I keep it tuned up all de time ready for de praise of de Lord Jesus. Oh, if I only could meet my ole master of de earth a comin' along the street some day, den de angels would have to minister de first rebuke in heaven, and say, 'Not quite so loud wid de music over in dat corner, for you disturb de children's meetin' on the Fourth Avenue.' But I fear I shall never meet him, for God says, dar shall in no wise enter into de city anything dat defiles, neither whatsoever works abomination or makes a lie, but dey which are written in de Lamb's book of life. He used to defile de women of de plantation and lead others to do the same, and do other immoral abominations—dar was no end to 'em, and den de matter was, he would cover it up and seem to be a saint on de Sunday. Oh, I fear his hopeless cries will never reach to de Throne. And yet some day one of de angels may come to me sayin' I have good news for you, your old master is at last earnestly prayin' and washin' hisself wid his tears and de soap of de word. Den dis ole harp would begin on de highest key, until de angel would have to say, 'Rastus, you had better drop back to de key of F, for he's a leper from de sole of his foot to de crown of his head, and will need to dip himself seven times in de Jordan afore he is clean.'"

"Well, Rastus," I said, how about the rest of the slaves, are many of them here in heaven?"

"Oh," he said, "dear Mr. Sodi, I 'spects you haven't recognized dem since they have put on their shinin' garments and put off de black ones—There's multitudes of dem here and dey sing in de choir wid de odder people and their voices are often de loudest. Of course, dey are not all here by any means.

"Many of dem were as big hypocrites as de master. Some were of de fearful kind; some of de unbelievin' sort, and some were de whoremongers and de liars. And God says all these shall have their part in de lake of fire and brimstone. If I could only go back and see dem once more, I would take dis harp and show dem dis robe, and take 'em one bunch of de fruit—dey might believe me, though dey would not believe Moses and de prophets."

"Well, Rastus, the visit has been very interesting to me."

"And to me also," said Rastus, "but my company is scattering and I must also go, and will see you again soon, I trust." So saying he said good-bye and disappeared among the chariots, and thousands who were leaving the martyrs' reunion.

I now said to mother, "It does seem a most blessed thing that there are no feelings of prejudice here toward anyone whom God sees fit to enter the gates."

"Oh," she said, "we are here from every nation under heaven, all races, kindreds, tongues and people are here, and all are in the likeness of their Lord, while all retain a peculiar likeness to their former life. But see David's chariot is coming." In a few moments we were seated with him and flying with great speed toward the city gate.

We passed in at the gate of Manasseh and at last stopped near the children's great Polytechnic. Mother and Mary stepped out and I said good-bye for now, saying, "I hope to see you again soon," for David had said, 'I will take you on a flying trip through some of the leading avenues toward the Throne, for I see your heart is in that direction and I have a commission to be your servant for a time.'

On we went through streets and avenues, flying at a tremendous speed. The light of the Throne began to be luminous in the distance, even the trees lining the thoroughfares, somewhat like the trees for shade in earthly cities, seemed hanging with diamonds and rubies of glistening brightness and the mansions seemed literally studded with the same.

We now came to a broad avenue leading toward the Throne. Thousands of glorified saints, some walking, engaged in holy conversation, others in the chariots, with the joy and rest of heaven upon them, were going to and from the Throne.

I now turned to David and said, "While I am eager to go on to the Throne, I am very eager to see the dear bosom companion of my life, who I am told is detained in a distant place in paradise."

"Oh," said David, "why did you not tell me while we were in paradise? We could have gone so quickly, but now I will turn the chariot, and go at once, for I know her well and she will be greatly pleased, and I myself will be greatly pleased in assisting you for this great pleasure trip." So turning his chariot, he said, "Have you any choice of routes?"

"Not any, for I know nothing of the way, only go past the children's Polytechnic and take mother and Mary. I am so ignorant of the ways, so choose for me."

"Most gladly indeed," said David. So with the speed of sound we were flying toward the great cathedral, and soon stopped beside the gate." [i]

97

* * *

I was eager to see my bosom companion who was busily engaged with a thousand more, as I had been told, assisting a great number of souls who had recently come into the heavenly realm from certain heathen countries where the missionaries had been busily preaching the Lord Jesus. So, as we were waiting in the chariot, I saw my mother and Mary passing near, and motioned them to come to us. When I told them of my great desire and David's pleasing offer, they at once accepted our invitation to go along with us and were soon seated by our side.

Mother at once said, "I know well where they are, at one of the remote locations far beyond the gate of Benjamin."

So David turned the chariot to the right, saying, "I will go down Ninety-second Avenue and out at the gate of Benjamin."

No sweeter raptures filled my soul since leaving the Judean gate at our first entrance into the city, and where we had been welcomed by the Lord of the kingdom. The thoughts of the family reunion were so precious. Mother and daughter by my side. David the sweet singer of Israel, our servant. He who had led the hosts of the servants of the Most High and fought His battles, now our servant and so soon to meet the dear wife of my youth who has for many years been so prominent in these eternal realms in service for her Lord. Oh, blessed morning it was to me! My whole soul was in raptures of delight with the sweet thought. David now said, "Are you ready?" and the chariot moved on. We were now passing through a new section of the city to me. Mother and Mary seemed to be much at home and acquainted with the route.

Mary now spoke and said, "Father, I am so glad you can so soon see dear mother, she has been so busy of late. She has not had time to visit with me, as we often do, but we will soon meet, and I can introduce you. I wonder if she will know you among all the busy crowd."

"Know me! Oh, yes. How could she help knowing me? I have changed but little since we parted. Indeed, dear child, I am very eager to see her myself, even more than you can know, for you have had no separations from any loved ones. Neither have you known the sorrows and tears which we have known so long. All these you escaped, as well as the dark sins of the world. I do not think now we ought to have grieved so much and so long as we did when you left us, for you were eternally safe from that moment."

"Oh, indeed, I am safe and very happy in my experience. I know nothing of the sorrow and tears of which you speak. Others have often told me of their sad mistakes and sin-burdened hearts: but how thankful they all are, for our blessed Redeemer! Without Him I would have been lost myself and would never have seen nor entered this celestial world."

David began to reduce the speed of the chariot, and, calling me by my name, said, "I want you to notice what we are now passing."

On both sides of the great avenue there were multitudes of peculiar, yet most beautifully constructed mansions.

"These," said David, "are built according to the tastes and fancies of their occupants, as indeed all the 'many mansions' are. You have noticed the great variety of scenery and buildings throughout the city, no doubt. Everyone can choose his own, and change to another at his own will. God Himself delights in variety and has made no two blades of grass alike, neither two grains of sand, nor two human souls. But communities in the world with similar choices—education and fancies—naturally group together here, so you see in these peculiar mansions. You will notice how happy and contented everyone seems to be in this great colony."

Mother now spoke and said to David, "I have been here for many years and yet I have never seen anyone dissatisfied or restless or homesick. It seems our great Father has anticipated all the wishes and desires of all His people and has so planned and arranged this eternal kingdom that everyone has his desires fully met in all things."

"The city," said David, "with all its variety of architecture and constructions, its fruits and rivers and fountains, is adapted to all the nations of the earth, and from all the nations, kindreds, people and tongues, these countless numbers are gathered. Multitudes from heathen nations are here, their children especially, in large numbers are here, for they do not arrive to the age of accountability so early as in Christian lands. These are all saved by virtue of the atonement, until they sin against eternal light, so thousands are gathered here well grown in years and it is these that are being taught, by these faithful servants, in the preparatory regions of paradise, to which point we are now going."

"Oh, David," I said, "will you drive your chariot faster, for I am eager to meet her who was the bosom companion of my life on earth?"

With this the chariot flew as with the speed of sound. The avenue was a perfect pleasure ground of delight. Trees loaded with their ripening fruit! Beautiful mansions of all descriptions! Thousands of happy souls, going and coming! Many reclining on the cushioned upholstery of heaven! But with the speed we were now going thousands of mansions were passed without distinguishing one from another.

"I see the gateway in the distance," said Mary.

"Are we so near the great wall and the entrance into paradise?" I said.

I looked up to scan the great wall again, with its magnificent splendors, as David was slowing his chariot. The gate stood open as indeed they all do. As we passed out at the gate of Benjamin with its great glistening pearl and shining hinges of gold, we had only time to cast one glance backward to say good-bye to the city, until we seemed to be a hundred kilometers[5] beyond, along one of the great highways of paradise.

Mary leaned her head upon my shoulder and said, "Father, how do you like the music and hum of the chariot wheels? Ordinarily they are almost noiseless."

"Oh, I am bewildered at the immensity and grandeur of heaven. Mother, how soon do you think we will reach our destination?"

"Oh, quite soon, I think I see the domes and steeples of the mission now."

"Yes," said Mary, "they are quite plain to me."

---

5. "Many leagues." That is maybe 50 miles. A league being about 5.7 kilometres (3.5 miles).

"Oh, glory!" I said. "Look at the mountains, hills, and valleys we are passing. Oh, my soul is perfectly full of rapture. Oh, for a thousand tongues —"

"Use the one you have," said Mary.

"Hallelujah to God!" I shouted, when David quickly took his harp and we all sang again the victories of the Lamb.

The chariot now stood still outside a great archway leading to one of the preparatory departments in paradise. We all stepped out when to my surprise more than a hundred most beautiful spirits met us, all with the glory and light of heaven upon them. Introduction? I needed none—especially to one—the fairest among the hundred, and altogether lovely. She sprang from among the rest and shouted, "Glory to God in the highest!" She hugged me tightly but could not weep, neither could I, for none can weep in heaven, but the cup of our joy was full.

"I knew you were coming," said Genevive, "but did not know David would bring you. Oh, how glad I am you are now at home! And then here's mother and daughter," she said, as she embraced them both in her arms.

"Dear Genevive, I have been so eager to see you ever since coming into paradise, but could not reach you earlier. Our dreams of the future while on earth are now realized, our prayers answered. Home at last!"

"Oh," said Genevive, "I have much to ask you, so we will walk to that group of buildings over there."

David said, "My time is at your disposal. Take your leisure, for so I have command."

As we walked slowly along I was introduced to many of those who met us at the gateway. I found they were from various parts of the world, but all were engaged in a blessed service for our Lord. Everyone seemed perfectly joyful and happy. [j]

*   *   *

We were now inside a most beautiful building—a large drawing room or parlor, beautifully decorated with various kinds of ornaments unlike what I was used to seeing within the gates of the city. Everything was tinged with silver drapings, lovely indeed, and the upholstery of chairs, sofas, etc., were of magnificent designs of heavenly patterns.

From this room we were brought into the large spacious dining hall which was practically ablaze with burnished silver hangings and all manner of silvertinged table ware. Think of a table one and a half kilometers long[6], at which ten thousand guests can sit down at one time and you have some idea of this dining hall.

Genevive now came and said, "We will go to the side table over there where we can sit down together." So Genevive, Mary, mother and myself were seated alone, while David and all who met us at the gate were gone on to the farther end of the great hall.

Genevive now ordered our luncheon which consisted of beautiful cakes of the finest of the wheat of paradise, with all manner of fruit with which paradise abounds everywhere. Breadfruit grows in abundance and is one of the twelve kinds on each tree. When our thanksgiving was over, Genevive, who sat by my side, said to me, "I have been eagerly waiting for this time to come when we would all be together again and the sorrows of earth be over. Now tell me about the rest of the children."

"Yes," said Mary, "tell us all about them. I am so eager to know about my brothers and sisters of whom mother says there are six."

"I am glad to tell you they are all alive and getting on well in the world and in homes of their own. They are not all good Christians and yet they have all known the way of life and we trust they will yet all be counted among the saved."

"Oh, yes," said Genevive, "I have so often prayed for them and that angel over there which you see with David and the rest, has often told me about them, for he often visits the sections of earth where they live."

"How often I have wondered with great curiosity, if the saints in heaven know about the affairs and doings of those they have left behind, and your words, Genevive, thoroughly convince me that they do."

---

6. "Three thousand cubits." That is about 4,500 feet, or about 1,371 meters. A cubit is about 18 inches.

"True, indeed," said Genevive, "we have frequent messages from the earth."

"Oh, Genevive, there is no comparison between the humble fare of our earthly table and what we have here. How refreshed I feel, and then those wonderful fountains in the distance, gushing up from burnished silver fixtures, and hundreds gathering about them drinking to their hearts' content! Oh, heaven, indeed! How precious that promise: 'He shall lead them to fountains of living water!'" (Revelation 7:17)

"This is its fulfillment," said Genevive, "and when you see the ten thousand at these tables with the bounties of heaven before them then you'll say, 'The Lamb which is in the midst of the Throne shall feed them,' (Revelation 7:17) for truly all this blessed provision and infinitely more than what we can see here, is the gracious result of His thoughtful care of His people, for He has prepared for them a city." (Hebrews 11:16)

"Now," said Mary to Genevive, "I wish you would take us through the great amphitheater."

We all arose and followed as Genevive led the way. A doorway opened from the great dining hall into a stupendous auditorium, furnished with seats somewhat like the ancient amphitheaters of the world. Thousands were seated in various places of this great building. Silver furnishings were everywhere sparkling with the glory of paradise. This great hall I found to be one of the places where the heathen are gathered who have been saved by Christ and are yet uninstructed in the ways of the kingdom or in spiritual matters in reference to salvation. One of the chief stations of paradise opening its doors to heathen countries is just near this place.

Genevive now said, "I always took a great interest in mission work in the world, in Sunday school and children's classes, and the same traits are with me here. Of my own choice I spend much time instructing the precious souls who come to these portals, ignorant of God's plans and purposes. All the heathen infants are saved as well as those in civilized and Christian lands. They don't reach accountability as early as they do in more enlightened nations, hence a larger number die in childhood and youth who have never known the law of God so as to bring them under condemnation. And being under the free gift of eternal life, they arrive here in very great surprise. While heathen nations are responsible to God, yet their responsibility is not so great as those of Christian lands."

"But, mother," said Mary, "how is it that so many of the heathen children are saved and gathered here when so many of their parents are lost?"

"Their parents," said Genevive, "have reached an age of accountability through the measure of light they have. They have likewise sinned and fallen under condemnation and following their superstitions have died in their sins, while their children have not reached the place of enlightenment to bring them under such responsibility."

At this I spoke and said, "The Bible declares that: 'By the transgression of one man judgment came upon all men to condemnation. Even so, by the righteousness of one man the free gift came upon all men to justification of life.' (Romans 5:18) So in man's beginning he is universally saved by Christ, as Paul said again, 'I was alive without the law once, but when the commandment came sin revived and I died.'" (Romans 7:9)

"Indeed," said Genevive. "All are alive and remain so until they receive a knowledge of God's will sufficient to bring them under responsibility, when by transgression spiritual death follows. But I see you are eager to know about this great place for the gathering of the multitudes of those saved by Christ from heathen lands. Do you notice what a large proportion are young people and children? These have had but little instruction in the ways of the true God, His worship and spiritual nature—many of them none at all. Their teaching of idolatry clings to them and they must be trained in the ways and truths of the eternal kingdom.

"Each of these has a history of its own. They wonder with great astonishment as to who and where they are, when the angels have brought them inside the gates of paradise. The shining glory of this world is so great, many of them are completely overcome, like one on earth just awakened from a sleep filled with an enchanting dream, they are speechless with wonder. Little children of different ages are here and yet many of these know as much as children of Christian lands. This great amphitheater is often filled until every seat is taken and here they are taught everything pertaining to an earlier experience in this world of light. Many of them were objects of scorn and neglect, without friends or a mother's love. They greatly admire and wonder at the kindness shown them here. Thousands and millions of them have gone throughout the regions of paradise and into the city and their voices are ringing out with the melody of heaven."

"Genevive," I said, "why is this place arranged for the heathen more than for any others?"

"It is not for heathen children alone," she replied. "There are many here from Christian lands, but God has made wise provisions for all His people. The teaching here is adapted to a class who hardly know the basic elements of anything in modern or civilized life, and who know nothing of the doctrines of salvation. Many of those boys and girls and even men and women whom you see are being taught in those classes over there, are only as those in the introductory class in the schools of the world. The great effort is to instruct them and develop their spiritual and intellectual faculties. It is most interesting to note how quickly they develop from mere babes into full-fledged saints in heaven.

"They all quickly learn to praise God and everyone has a harp similar to your own. The great praise services which are held here very frequently are soul-refreshing seasons, I assure you. When twenty thousand to thirty thousand all join in the new songs so recently learned, and quoting passages and heavenly teaching concerning the eternal truths of God, much as we did on earth in our praise services, these arches and domes echo and re-echo the melody until you would think the vibrations would be heard in the city itself."

"Well, Genevive, I cannot tell you how much I have enjoyed this meeting and visit with you. My whole soul is filled with the highest sense of adoring praise to our Lord, for such love tokens for His people. Surely, all these great things for the children He had in mind before the foundation of the world was laid."

"Indeed," said Genevive, "or even before this paradise was planned or fitted up."

"Well, dear Genevive, are you engaged here so constantly that you cannot go to other places when you would like to do so?"

"Oh, no," she replied, "I have the most unbounded freedom, even as that of the angels or the elders themselves, to go as I will, and I will be exceedingly glad to accompany you to any places you wish to go."

"Oh, Genevive, nothing could give me more pleasure than to have you go with us. I was just planning a visit to the Throne itself when I felt I must see you first and David generously offered his services and our party was quickly made up, as you see."

"If you would like," said Genevive, "I will go with you to the Throne and we can return at our leisure to this or other parts of paradise." So she called mother and Mary to us and made the proposition which was quickly accepted. She dispatched one standing nearby to bring David and the hundred, and in a few moments they were with us.

I said to David, "We have decided to return at once to the city and to go on toward the Throne."

"I am at your pleasure until this trip is ended."

Genevive quickly arranged for others to fill her place in the great preparatory classes, saying we must now join with the rest in a chorus of thanksgiving, before we leave the amphitheater. The order of the services was quickly arranged; David led in the chorus. We had tuned our harps and joined with them, and falling on our faces, with adoring praises, we practically shouted the salvation of God. We now arose and with deep emotions said good-bye to the great multitude we were leaving behind. We walked toward the gateway where stood the chariot. After saying once again good-bye to those beautiful spirits of light, with the pure love tokens of which heaven abounds, we were seated in the chariot. [k]

CHAPTER EIGHT
On to the Throne [1]

avid now said, "Have you a choice of routes? Six thousand kilometers[7] are between us and the city gates."

Genevive quickly spoke and said, "Let us go by way of the gorge route including the cliffs, for I remember Mr. Sodi was very fond of natural scenery and especially that of a mountainous and inspiring character."

"I am sure, father, you will have your desire fully met," said Mary. "I do not know what the world was like or its mountains and rivers, but I have gone this route a few times with mother and grandmother, as well as others, and I know you will be pleased."

"Indeed, I am sure I will. And Genevive, dear, I am glad you remember my natural inclinations and have made this choice, for I still have my same preferences."

David's chariot began to tremble as a thing of life again. We turned to the many standing at the gateway and said good-bye, until we meet you again.

I found that Genevive had a host of friends, for thousands had gathered to see her off, and to sing a parting hymn; the chorus I still remember:

---

7. "A thousand leagues." That is 3,500 miles. A league being about 5.7 kilometres (3.5 miles).

"We only say good-bye in heaven,
Assured to meet again.
God's blessing guide you all the way
By mountain, vale, or glen."

As the chariot moved away, they soon faded from our sight in the distance behind. Beautiful fields with teeming harvests were spread out in a great valley before us.

Mother spoke, and said, "Not a drop of human sweat was needed to produce these fields of golden harvests. There is no curse here—no weeds nor briars, but our good Father's will makes all provision for us. Yet notwithstanding everything grows in heaven without human toil and sweat, yet men are employed to gather in these great harvests and the labor is but a kind of picnic for joy."

"Oh, how much," I replied, "is wrapped up in God's love to man!" Beautiful flowers of endless varieties were lining the chariot's pathway. "The fragrance from the fields and flowers is so exhilarating, my soul is filled with raptures of delight," I shouted. Oh, why do men in the world put so little value on God's revelation of this great pleasure ground of eternal delight?

Many Christian people there are who try to believe that heaven is only a state of rest and quietude of soul forever, and do not think of it as a place of such magnificent glory. Such rob themselves of the joy of expectation, and hope is not the anchor it would be if their faith and hope were after God's ideas and revelations.

We now came in sight of beautiful buildings in the distance. So I said to Genevive, "What are those buildings we see over there?"

"Just a village of paradise," she said. "Many of the inhabitants have mansions also in the city, but often spend much of their lime here, as these pleasure grounds are greatly appreciated."

David reduced the speed of the chariot as we passed through its streets. Beautiful fountains were beside the driveway and so were the trees with their ripening fruit.

David stopped beside a gushing fountain; we all sprang from the chariot and with silver goblets were refreshed with the water of life. After selecting such fruit as we needed we were again in the chariot, which moved on with reduced speed, for the scenery was too grand to be so quickly passed by.

Soon the hills and mountains far in the distance before us came in view. A lovely river winding about the foothills was also plain to be seen. On we passed. Deep gorges between the hills and spurs of the mountains lent their enchantment to the scene. The roadway was now winding among this gorgeous mountain scenery. The chariot was climbing the mountain sides, so as to pass over the high mountain valleys.

David now turned to me and said, "My son, I am delighted to have this opportunity of driving through this stupendous mountain route, nor do I ever tire of it. It reminds me when I used to hide in the caves and among the rocks and mountains when fleeing from Saul, my persecutor. Those were times never to be forgotten. I have often looked but in vain hoping I might see Saul coming in a chariot along some of the great mountain roads of paradise, but I have never met him nor have I heard any word concerning his presence within the gates of paradise or the city itself."

"Poor Saul," I said. "He rejected God's word and denied obedience to Him, and the penalty must be paid."

I now looked up to the vast overhanging crags above us and again downward to the deep gorges of thousands of feet below. At different places along this roadway were beautiful pleasure grounds so whenever or wherever any desired, they could alight from the chariot and enjoy strolls among beautiful shrubbery and all manner of trees bearing fruit. At one of these David brought the chariot to a standstill, and we all gathered beneath the wide spreading branches of one of the trees of life and began to gather its fruit. I felt so full of thanksgiving to God that I practically shouted, "What has God made! Oh, David, tell me, how vast is this great paradise?"

"Oh," said David, "there is plenty of room in heaven for all the millions that ever have been or ever will be born. These pleasure grounds are almost limitless. I do not know the utmost bounds of heaven: possibly Enoch, Abraham or Moses can tell. One thing I can tell: there is no sin, no sorrow, nor death here. There is no evil-minded person in all this vast domain. Nothing that works an abomination or makes a lie ever enters within the gates of the city or even paradise itself."

At this David went to the chariot and bringing his harp said, "We must now join in a song of thanksgiving." We quickly took our harps from our belts and tuned them with David's. He began with the word of the thirty-third Psalm, thinking I knew it best. Then we all sang:

> "Rejoice in the Lord, O ye righteous:
> for praise is comely for the upright.
>
> Praise the Lord with harp:
> sing unto Him with the psaltery
> and an instrument of ten strings.
>
> Sing unto Him a new song:
> play skillfully with a loud noise.
> For the word of the Lord is right,
> and all His works are done in truth.
>
> By the word of the Lord
> were the heavens made,
> and all the host of them
> by the breath of His mouth."

When we had finished this song of thanksgiving, David said, "No doubt, you will meet Nehemiah, one of the dear saints of heaven, who wrote while on earth, as I remember, under divine inspiration, and said: 'You, even you are Lord alone; you have made heaven, the heaven of heavens, with all their hosts; the earth and all things that are therein, the sea and all that is therein, and you preserve them all, and the hosts of heaven worship you.'" (Nehemiah 9:6)

He continued, "Angels from this heavenly world visit the earth in great numbers and sometimes saints have the privilege as well, but of this I will speak to you at another time."

"Oh, how blessed to know," I replied, "that I belong to Him: that I was converted, became as a little child, believed in Jesus, humbled myself, was born again, received eternal life, and now have this great exaltation! Oh, hallelujah to God!" I shouted.

Genevive said, "Shall we not now go on, for there are many things yet on the way to the city?"

We were soon seated in the chariot and David touched the special button and the chariot moved along, rolling on in the mighty ascent toward the mountain summit. Off in the distance could be seen peak after peak and mountain after mountain— everything glittering with the glory of God upon it. Still we moved on and climbed higher and higher, spanning immense gorges on causeways built by the Lord of the Kingdom Himself.

To one unaccustomed, it seemed both a dizzy and dangerous route. I said to Genevive, "Are we entirely safe with such enormous heights, and such speed as we are making?"

"Safe?! Dangerous route?!" she said. "There are no dangers in heaven. Accidents, there are none. Mistakes are few as we soon learn the deeper wisdom of God."

We passed many chariot loads going in the direction from whence we had just come. All were so cheerful and happy. We always gave and received a pleasant salute as the chariots passed each other with reduced speed. Nearly always the newcomers like myself would shout out with a wave of the hand, 'Home at last, home at last!'

We met one chariot upon the summit of this great range, guided by Elijah, filled with men and women with a half dozen children besides new arrivals from the world, but a happier group I hardly ever saw. David threw out a signal and both chariots stood still side by side. We greeted each other with handshakes and kisses of true love. The children were so full of glee and joyous wonder. Like myself, this was their first trip over this wonderful gorge route. They asked us many questions and seemed eager to go on. No thought of fear, but with perfect confidence in their elders, and Elijah's guiding hand, they seemed entirely satisfied. After passing them a basket of fruit which we had gathered, they thanked us and their chariot moved on.

David said, "Now we must hurry on for there are interesting things just before us." So on we went, climbing still higher. We soon came to a most lovely park on the plateau high upon the mountain summit. Into this park David guided his chariot. We

sat a moment awestruck at the lovely scenery. Groves of heavenly
fruit-bearing trees, flowering shrubbery of many kinds, roadways
winding in all directions, with a great number of chariots much
like David's standing here and there, with others slowly moving
about filled with joyous souls—men, women and children—all
happy and enjoying this heavenly pleasure ground to the full.

"Sure enough," I said. "What has God prepared for His
people!?"

David now brought his chariot to a halt. Many of the great
host turned toward us, recognizing David, the king. In a few
moments a great company had gathered near, saluting David
and us. But, who are the strangers, they wondered. We were
soon introduced and greeted afresh. David now said, "Take your
leisure, go where you wish."

We took a long stroll, meeting hundreds who like myself were
here for the first time. The great pleasure park was three or four
kilometers[8] on each side. Numerous fountains were located at
different places and were the sources of innumerable rivers and
streams in paradise, and a part of the great system which flows
from the city and from the Throne itself on the banks of which,
both in the holy city and throughout all paradise, grow the trees
of life with their twelve manner of fruit. A table in the center was
literally covered with this delightful fruit of paradise of which we
all ate freely, while enjoying this most interesting visit.

"Well, my son," said mother, "are you repaid for your efforts
and self-denial in the Lord's service in the world?"

"Oh, mother, why do you ask me that question? I am a
thousand times repaid already. Just what I see and enjoy now
here in this park is ample reward for all the toil of an earth's
pilgrimage. But who are those two men coming toward us?"

Mother said, "I do not recognize them."

Genevive said, "They are strangers, perhaps recently come
into paradise." By this time they were near us. They had locked
arms and were walking together in a joyous conversation.

They attracted my attention, for I seemed to recognize them
both. "Hello, good morning," and in a moment we were embracing

---

8. "Fifteen or twenty furlongs." That is about two to two and a half miles.
One furlong being about 200 meters (660 feet).

each other in our arms and with high praises to God we were shouting, "Glory to God in the highest!" But who were they? Only two of my friends whom I had learned to know and to love many years ago, one Mr. Fuggele of Stavanger, Norway, and the other dear soul was my friend Mr. Ransome, of London, England.

"Oh, brethren," I shouted, "I see you are here, but I had not heard that you had left the world. Oh, Brother Fuggele, the last time we met on earth, we wept together in the railroad station in your native town, and Brother Edwin Ransome, you were a father to me when I was in your great city of London. Well, brethren, I am truly glad to meet you here. I have only been here a short time and have not yet been to the Throne, but oh, I am overwhelmed with the greatness and glory of this celestial world."

Edwin Ransome now said, "We have been here for quite a while, but never have been to this great pleasure ground before. Isn't it grand?"

"This beats the mountains of Norway," said Brother Fuggele. "I thought they were grand enough, although snow covered and frozen with the ice like the frigid zone, in mid-summer, but here the enormous heights of these delightful mountains know nothing but the spring mornings of heaven. Surely, no cold blasts ever sweep over these mountain tops."

"No," I shouted, "for just see these trees of giant growth, hanging with their golden fruits, like the luxuriant clusters of the tropical lands of the earth. No winter ever comes here, I am sure."

At this there came a group of happy men, precious souls, passing near us. I said, "Who are they?" and they were quickly invited to wait a moment for an introduction.

My friends Edwin Ransome and Peter Fuggele knew them well and said, "They are a group of ministers who were noted and well-known in the world, greatly beloved on earth and so they are in heaven."

I was soon introduced to Christmas Evans and Rowland Hill of England, Dr. Guthrie also. Robert Flockhart and John Wesley stood side by side. Dr. Adam Clark and George Fox were also introduced, then there came Peter Cartwright and Lorenzo Dow, with many others.

"Oh," I exclaimed and said, "I have heard and read of all you good men. Glad indeed, very glad I am to meet you all here. This must be the 'preachers' picnic party.'" I motioned to mother, Genevive and Mary, who also came and were introduced. A number of seats were brought and placed beneath the broad, spreading branches of the tree and we all sat down, when we saw David coming toward us carrying his harp. When he had come near, all these brethren arose and greeted him with a most heavenly welcome. David made a most courteous bow and with a pleasant smile was seated with us. Then standing and taking in the situation, he quickly introduced his chariot group again when they arose and gave us another welcome. At this I arose and said, "Dear brethren, my soul is so overcome with the joy and gladness of heaven, I can no longer restrain my feelings."

"Don't try any longer," said Rowland Hill, "but let us all praise God together." We knelt, and such a praise service I hardly ever witnessed, especially of such intense feelings and raptures of joy. George Fox seemed to praise God louder and sweeter than most anyone else. At last we arose and David started a hymn, playing upon his harp. We all joined and sang with him. After much conversation we decided that all would go together to the farther side of the park. David led the way and we all followed. We soon found that many of these blessed men had not visited this place nor passed over this route for a long time so it seemed as new to them as to us.

Again I said to Genevive, "I am glad you chose this route for our return trip to the city. Oh, such glorious things as are in store for us!" We soon came to the outer limits of the park where we found ourselves on the very summit of a great mountain range in paradise. As we stood and looked off in the far distance over the foothills and down through immense valleys and plains, we seemed lost in wonder. In the beautiful clear atmosphere of heaven we could see great distances over and into the valleys a hundred kilometers[9] below us. The roadways winding down the mountain side with such a variety of trees on their borders presented a scene before us without a parallel in all creation. As I stood looking over this wonder, I said to David with the

---

9. "Many leagues." That is maybe 50 miles. A league being about 5.7 kilometres (3.5 miles).

words of the Queen of Sheba, "The half has never been told me," (1 Kings 10:7) and again, "Eye has not seen, nor ear heard, neither has it entered into the heart of man, the things which God has prepared for them that love him." (1 Corinthians 2:9) As we looked far down into the valley as well as along the mountain slopes we could see an innumerable number of mansions and temporary residences of those who preferred to spend much of their time in those regions. I thought again of our Lord's words: "I go to prepare a place for you, that where I am, there ye may be also," (John 14:2-3) and oh, what provision He has made!

Genevive now came and said, "Mr. Sodi, is your curiosity satisfied?"

"Satisfied! Is any soul not satisfied here? I have climbed to the top of many of the highest mountains of the earth, but they were only mole hills compared to these wonders of paradise, and then just think, these are here forever. Ours to enjoy always! No sickness! No old age! No death, sorrow nor crying! Redeemed and saved forever! Oh, Genevive, I am so glad we are here! Oh what glorious heights of elevation to which we are raised! Only a little while ago we were in the world subject to sickness, sorrow and death. Now all this is passed. No more death! But in heaven, equal to the angels, and with the saved of all ages!"

David now came and said, "We have need to be on our journey," and so, bidding our holy brethren good-bye, we returned to the chariot. After gathering our needed supply of fruit and drinking again from the gushing fountain we were quickly seated in David's chariot prepared for our journey to the city of the great King. We sung a hymn of praise for these great wonders. As soon as we had begun to sing many hundreds gathered quickly when they saw David standing in the chariot with his harp and joined with us in loud hallelujah's to God.

Just at this moment came two lovely women, inviting us to wait a little and dine with them at their table nearby. They knew David well and asked concerning us; we quickly introduced ourselves, when Mary recognized them both and sprang from the chariot and embraced them in her arms, saying, "Oh, Emma dear, and Susie, how glad I am to see you!" These, I found had been her companions in their infancy in heaven. "Oh," she says, "father, these were my chums in our girlhood experiences." Of course, we went with them for they knew David also.

They, like ourselves, were just picnicking for a brief time on this mountain summit. They had gathered many kinds of fruit and a beautiful table was loaded with all that any soul could wish. Surely we enjoyed this feast as souls only can who have passed the boundaries of earthly lives into the new unions and fellowships of the life eternal. We thanked them for the pleasant entertainment and bidding them good-bye were soon in the chariot again.

* * *

So the chariot moved on leaving the mountain scenery behind us. Our route now was through a broad but beautiful valley. We could see such great distances before us in the clear light of paradise. The great orchards, orange and lemon groves of the world, were but miniature garden spots to what now opened before us.

As we made our descent from the heights behind us there was spread out as far as the eye could reach on either side immense groves of fruit-bearing trees of all kinds and descriptions, interspersed with most lovely flowers such as I had never seen before.

"Oh, where are we?" I shouted. "I am bewildered with this magnificent glory and wonderful provision of our God." I fell on my face. Genevive and Mary both joined me and blessed aloud the God of our being. "Oh, God, Maker of all! Oh, Lord Jesus, Redeemer and Saviour, with high thanksgiving we pour out our souls to You! Eternal praise shall be Yours forever."

When we arose, my mother said, "From these regions vast supplies are taken into the city. Look," said she, "at those trainloads over there."

"Wonderful," I said, as I saw hundreds busily loading them with the choicest fruit and spiritual vegetables of all kinds.

Six hundred kilometers[10] of these groves were passed. I saw

---

10. "A hundred leagues." That is about 350 miles. A league being about 5.7 kilometres (3.5 miles).

many thousands of happy spirits gathering fruit from these orchards of beauty and trainloads were frequently leaving, headed for the city.

Genevive now said, "Do you see the light of the city over there?"

"Oh, indeed," I shouted. "I think it must be the sunrise of a June morning in heaven."

"How well you have judged," said David. "The Son of God, the Lamb Himself, is the light thereof. June morning always! There is no winter here." In a few moments the wall of the city came into view, and the gate of Simeon loomed up before us.

"Oh, David, reduce your speed, give us more time to see and consider the greatness of this mighty wall, and to read again the names of the foundations on which it stands, before we pass in at the gate of Simeon."

The angel of the gate threw up his hands with a lovely welcome. I said to Genevive, "Why do the angels guard the gateways bearing the names of the twelve tribes of Israel?"

"Oh," said she, "had it not been for the twelve tribes of ancient Israel paving this way before us and giving us the alphabet, spelling the eternal mysteries of God, we would never have known such an abundant entrance into the city. But like Israel when plodding their way to their ancient capital and the annual feasts, we would have been no better prepared than they, and with the increasing numbers gathering at these gates they would be blocked and jammed to our utter confusion. So the angel is stationed just to guide the crowds, to preserve perfect order, and to welcome all who are prepared for the blessedness of the city and the mansions. Ignorance is no bar to entrance at the gates but an unlikeness to the blessed face of Jesus is. So the angel's presence and judgment decides."

"So," said Genevive, "ancient Israel opened the way and went before all of us Gentiles. God had prepared for them a city and they looked forward with longing eyes toward their inheritance."

"Oh, indeed, Genevive dear, I remember a precious word of the Bible which we used to love so much while on earth. Speaking of Abraham, it says: 'For he looked for a city which has foundations whose builder and maker is God.'" (Hebrews 11:10)

40 Days in Heaven

"How true," said Genevive, "these ancient saints died in faith, full of the promises of God, which they saw afar off. And they were persuaded of them and embraced them and so confessed they were strangers and pilgrims in the earth, desiring a better country, that was this heavenly one. So God was not ashamed to be called their God because He had built for them this city." (Hebrews 11:13-16)

"Oh, how true!" I said. "And none but the true and eternal God could have build such a city as this for them and us."

David's chariot had been standing still for some time during this conversation and he had been quietly listening. He now turned to us and said, "I have been delighted with the course of your conversation. For hundreds of years before the Gentile period came in, thousands of the Jews crowded at these gates.

"We were most all Jews then, but now the Gentiles are far outnumbering us. But then the Gentiles are our brethren for they are Abraham's seed after all and heirs of the promise. But we must now pass along." The chariot moved slowly under the archway of the great gate. The angel waved us good-bye as we left the wondrous gate and wall behind.

Mother now spoke and said to David, "Kindly guide the chariot to the children's cathedral."

I said to her, "Are you eager to see the little ones again?"

"I am always delighted to be with them, but I want to assure you I have greatly enjoyed this entire trip." We all said the same, but no one had enjoyed it like myself—everything was so new, so wonderful, never to be forgotten.

"Now, David, the avenue seems broad here, go as fast as you want to." He reached out his hand and pressed the button again, when the chariot seemed to fly with the wings of the light. In a few moments we were slowing up beside the gateway of the Polytechnic. We all alighted and thanked David for his kind services, who turned and said, "I am always glad to do you such a favor."

David now moved his chariot to the further side of the street and was gathering some fruit, while we were busy talking over the wonderful journey we had just completed." [m]

CHAPTER NINE
Meeting Jonah and Many Other Elders

enevive, mother and Mary were standing at the gateway. David's chariot was standing on the opposite side of the avenue, where he was still gathering some fruit and filling a basket. I saw Bohemond also coming toward us, and motioned to him to hurry.

"Oh, Bohemond, I have many things to tell you. Many blessed things have occurred since we parted. I want to introduce to you my bosom companion, the wife of my youth, whom I have just found most busily engaged in a distant part of paradise."

Genevive seemed greatly pleased to know we were such close friends.

Bohemond now said, "When are you going on to the Throne?"

"Oh, very soon, I trust."

Genevive spoke and said, "If you like, you can go on at once, and mother, Mary and myself will meet you at the great convocation a little later."

So we waved to David to come to us. He quickly consented to be our servant again, and we planned to be off. As we were exchanging good-byes, Genevive said to David, "Go by way of the mansions of the prophets and call at the mansion of Jonah."

"Oh, Genevive," I said, "how kind and thoughtful you are for me," and after pressing my lips to hers, with a good-bye kiss, as we used to do in the world, we were soon in the chariot which was heading toward the interior of the city. Ever since stepping from the chariot at my first entrance into paradise, this had been the goal of my constant desire, to reach and see my Father's Throne, for I remembered we are to reign with Him. I have already repeatedly seen our blessed Lord and looked into His holy face—but oh, I so very much want to see His Father's Throne and the multitudes that must be gathering about it.

"All your desires and more," said David, "will soon be granted you, but you have been wise in not hurrying to the Throne, for even now you are none too well prepared for its exceeding glory. Your trip into paradise will only better prepare you for the scenes just ahead for it is better further on."

Bohemond spoke and said, "I have been very busily engaged in various parts of the city since I saw you last, but I am exceedingly thankful of this opportunity of going along with you."

"Now David, tell us about the mansions of the prophets of which Genevive spoke."

"I will be only too glad to tell you about them. Very many of the prophets and ancient men of Israel, including the Patriarchs, had their mansions located near together. They are so grouped that they have easy and ready access to each other. These they call their own and yet everyone has perfect privilege to go and come as he likes. It is thought no intrusion here to come and stay as long as one desires. Everything in the city belongs to each of us—we are heirs of it all."

"Oh," I said, "has God prepared all these great things for me? Are they really mine?"

"As sure as you are in the city they are yours," said David.

"I do remember the scripture," I replied, "where God says: 'All are yours and ye are Christ's and Christ is God's.'" (1 Corinthians 3:22-23)

Bohemond spoke and said, "I am wondering about a mansion for myself and its location."

David replied and said, "Be patient, my son, God will settle you to your own satisfaction. But remember, you have unbounded privileges in the entire kingdom of heaven, both in the city and paradise. Go where you will. Come when you please, and be forever contented."

Like all the avenues and streets of the city this one was most gorgeously decorated. A branch of the river was flowing in the midst of it. On either side were growing the trees of life interspersed with many varieties of most beautiful shrubbery. No earthly camera ever made a picture even to compare to this heavenly glory.

Since leaving the children's Polytechnic our chariot had been rolling along with indescribable speed. Many dozens of kilometers[11] had been passed while Bohemond and I had been talking over the experiences of each since we had parted.

"Now," said David, "we are coming near to the mansions of the ancients." And reducing his speed he said, "You can recognize the names of many of the occupants no doubt, for all who are acquainted with Jewish history will be familiar with many of the names you see there." Sure enough, upon the doors and posts of the verandas and other places were the names of many of the ancient saints of God.

"Now," said David, "they are always glad to welcome all the new arrivals, as well as their old friends."

I said to David, "Genevive spoke of Jonah the prophet, will we pass his mansion?"

"Oh, yes, indeed," said David, and in a few minutes the chariot stopped near the threshold of a beautiful palace.

"Well, I see the prophet's name," said Bohemond.

"To be sure," said David, "and he is the real Jonah of the Bible. I am also trusting for you, dear brethren, that he is now in his residence."

We all jumped from the chariot, and David leading the way, we were soon at the threshold. There are no door bells to ring in heaven, for everyone is always welcome. As well might a busy bee ask admission into its own hive as for one saint in heaven to have to ask another to admit him to his mansion, for there is an eternal brotherhood in heaven, with all things in common, as we know but little of on earth.

---

11. "Many hundred furlongs." That is tens of miles. One furlong being about 200 meters (660 feet).

We rejoiced exceedingly when David said, "I see Jonah now through the hallway over there."

As we entered his mansion, he came toward us and David saluted him with, "Good morning, my brother."

"Good morning to you," said Jonah. "I am always glad to have you come in. Tell me who are these brethren with you?"

"Recent arrivals. Brother Sodi is a Greek of Jewish descent but later from the Scandinavian people, and Bohemond from northern Russia."

"Glad to welcome you, dear brethren," he said, as he gave us his hand. We were soon all seated in his spacious mansion, beautiful with adornments as no earthly home has ever been decorated. As I looked around me I thought of our Lord's words on earth: "I go to prepare a place for you." (John 14:2) Oh, these many mansions, prepared by an almighty hand! Then I thought again, if He has made such an endless variety of flowers, sweet scented and lovely shrubbery of all kinds, with so many things to please and enhance our earthly lives, what will He not provide for His saints and His bride in heaven?

"Well, Jonah," I said, "we are glad to meet you indeed, but tell me, are you the prophet Jonah, so conspicuous in Bible times on earth?"

"I am the Prophet Jonah, son of Amittai, reared up in Gath Hepher, a town of old lower Galilee in Zebulun, more than two thousand seven hundred years ago—but that is reckoning like we used to on earth, but, dear brethren, it has really only been about two and one-half days since I came into this heavenly kingdom, reckoning by heaven's count.

"Well, do tell us, Jonah, of your experience with the whale. There has been a lot of skepticism about the story."

"The story is all true," said Jonah. "How I lived in the midst of the great fish I cannot tell. I only know I did live the three days inside the fish. But he was fully as sick of the job as I was myself. I have been asked these same questions thousands of times. It is an old story to me, yet ever new and ever true because God's hand was present both to punish and to save. My continued disobedience would have meant Nineveh's destruction, but my repentance and faithfulness meant their salvation. Yes, the story is true, whatever scoffers may say, miracle indeed it was—but it was followed by the greatest revival any city ever knew. My punishment and repentance was a sign to the Ninevites. They repented, God had mercy, and I was angry, oh, sinful Jonah that I was, but He had mercy on me also, and many of the Ninevites were saved and are now in heaven."

"Oh, Jonah," I exclaimed, "I wish you could only go back and repeat your story on earth again. Many skeptics are ridiculing the word of God over your experience."

"Yes," said Jonah, "and they will do it to their own destruction. Many great and strange things have occurred and will yet occur—some of them so strange that men will still doubt and object as they always have; nevertheless they are true."

"True indeed," I replied, "we have known children and animals born with two heads on opposite ends of one body, a peculiar working of some law of God producing what we called monstrosities. When other things strange occur in the physical realm, we say a miracle has occurred, and then men object and deny. But we are glad indeed to have met you and heard your story from your own lips. We have always believed God's word was true. Our Lord made reference to you eight hundred years after your time on earth, making you a sign of His own death and resurrection."

"Yes," said Jonah, "and it was all true, and skeptical men who were plentiful in the days of the Lord on earth, will stand at the last judgment day with the same men of Nineveh, while the Ninevites cry out against them. So will it be with latter days skeptics, who have abundantly more light than even the men in our Lord's time."

David spoke and said, "In my time many great things occurred. The hand of God was daily stretched out over me, and many deliverances He gave me—enough to fill a volume. Men in my time on earth generally accepted these special providences as God's hand in dealing with the affairs of men."

"Quite true," said Jonah, "for in my time some two hundred years after your death, everybody seemed to speak of you as one whom God greatly honored."

"Well, Jonah, we are going on to the Throne, and I am very eager to behold the glory of that most wonderful place in heaven about which we have sung and prayed all our earthly lives, and just think, I am so near to it now! Oh, hallelujah to my God! My soul is so full of raptures I cannot contain myself longer."

"Tune your harps," said David.

"Sure," I replied, and in a moment we were singing at the top of our voices, "The wonders of our God, our King."

"Oh, just think, we are in heaven, and really in the mansion of Jonah, the prophet, near to the Throne."

"It has been such a pleasure to me," said Jonah, "to meet you dear brethren who have lived on earth nearly three thousand years after my time, that now we must join with you in thanksgiving to God."

So at this we all fell on our faces with adoring praises to God.

When we had arisen, Jonah said, "I hope to be at the Throne during the great convocation. Millions of saints attend. I hope to meet you again at that time." So offering to us his hand, we all said good-bye to him, and were soon in David's chariot headed for the great center of the heavenly kingdom.

I said to David, "Are we not almost as near the Throne as we were when we turned back for the trip in paradise?"

"Quite as near," said David, "but we are approaching it from another direction this time."

The light seemed so bright, yet not dazzling, for we were being prepared for it. Thousands of happy souls were passing us. Many loads were being made up at different points arranging for the great convocation.

"Now," said David, "we must stop, for I see an angel calling to me." He sprang out of his chariot, and, after a few minutes conversation with the angel, came and said to us that he would have to leave us here for a little season, as he was called to a distant part of the city. "I think I shall leave you for only a little time. You can enjoy yourselves in such strolls as you like. Call at any of the mansions you wish. Feel perfectly at home. All you see is yours. I have to make a quick visit to a distant part of the city on business matters concerning the great convocation. If I do not return in time for you, step on any of the chariots and you will be taken to the Throne in due time." So saying we stepped from the chariot, he said good-bye to us with a lovely bow and wave of his hand, and his chariot had gone. [n]

* * *

Soon after leaving David's chariot, Bohemond and I were walking alone in a deep consideration of these great marvels, and the almightiness and love of God, when we came to a lovely park into which we entered. We had not gone far until we came upon a group of the elders, among whom were Abraham and Moses, Joshua and Isaiah, Peter and John, Paul and Silas, and many others. They were engaged in a spirited conversation. They motioned us to them, saying, "We are glad to meet you again, for we are informed that our Lord has gracious intentions concerning you."

"Well, holy brethren, we do not know what is before us, but we have found that He is full of infinite mercies and we are greatly interested in all we behold."

"We are very glad," said Abraham, "you have been wisely guided to this conference, and I have known of the extent of your visit up to this time, but we were just beginning a conversation on theology as it is now taught in the churches on earth, and if you are interested, we would invite you to remain for a time with us, and you are free to ask, and answer, any question you like."

We both spoke at once and accepted their kind invitation, for not often would one meet with so many men, so able as these, and the very ones who had contributed more for the faith of the church than others.

Abraham now said, "We are deeply interested in all the affairs of the church on earth, more so perhaps than those who still are in their earthly habitations and you have so recently come from the earth, we are glad to have you with us at this time."

"Indeed, we feel it a great privilege," I replied, "to sit with you in this conference."

At this, Moses passed to us a basket of most delicious fruit of which they had been partaking. Then Abraham spoke and said, "The theology which deals with the existence, character, and attributes of God, His laws and government, the doctrines men are to believe, and the duties they are to practice, has been much neglected in recent years, and we are informed that in many branches of the church grave errors have crept in."

"Religion," said he, "is the life of man in personal communication with God. It is the recognition of God in all of our duties. It is the bond which unites man to God. It is that faith which comprehends His presence, and invites Him into all the affairs of man's life. It is the life of God in the soul of man manifesting itself daily in practical morality."

"What then," I asked, "is the difference between religion and theology?"

"Religion," said Abraham, "has reference to God in the heart and life of man, which sows itself in obedience to all the divine will."

"Theology," said Moses, "is a scientific system, which deals with God and the laws by which man is saved. Yet a man may be a theologian, as were many of the Scribes and Pharisees, without religion based on experience. The source of all true theology is God Himself in the revelations He has given to man."

Paul then spoke and said, "These revelations are both natural and supernatural. Natural theology deals with God and His attributes as taught by nature. Nearly nineteen hundred years ago I wrote: 'For the invisible things of Him from the creation of the world are clearly seen, being understood by the things that are made, even His eternal Godhead, so they are without excuse.' (Romans 1:20) But the Scriptures," said he, "are the true source of correct theological teachings among men on the earth. They are a divinely inspired revelation to men. The careful interpretation of them reveals God to men as we have found Him after hundreds of years' acquaintance with Him here. They reveal His true nature, attributes, relations to and dealings with man. True theology deals also with man, his relations and duties to God and his fellow men, of the future state, which we are all now enjoying, with its rewards, and also the punishments which are dealt to the unrepentant."

At this, I spoke and said, "There has been much criticism and critical fault-finding of the Scriptures in the last few decades of time, so that I am glad of the privilege of asking you, who wrote so much of them, further concerning them, as to their authenticity, genuineness and authority as coming from God to man."

Moses was first to speak. He said, "Many scoffers and fault-finders were in my own time. No proof could satisfy them. There are mysteries of revelation as well as in the outward creation. I knew I was called and directly commissioned of God, and the books of the law were written by His express commandment. Joshua was my successor and went forth to his responsible task by appointment of our divine Lord, and his messages and writings were prefaced by such words as, 'Thus saith the Lord God of Israel.' Samuel, the prophet and seer of Israel, was early called of God and spake the word with authority from heaven. All the books of the prophets are composed of direct messages from God. Our Lord who sent us forth, fully recognized the whole body of our writings, included in the Old Testament Scriptures. He paid the highest honors to those ancient records, as He has fully told me. His seal being set to them they will stand forever. You need have no fears of the Scriptures ever falling beneath the feet of the church, on account of the efforts of skeptical men. God reserves to Himself the power to cause the earth to open its mouth again and swallow up the alliances of evil men, as in the days of Korah, Dathan and Abiram."

"Indeed," said Paul. "Our Lord put His full sanction to every jot and tittle of the law and the prophets and enforced the precepts written by Moses as binding upon all the Jewish people. He quoted the writings of nearly every prophet, from Moses to Malachi, recognizing their full authority, as the word of God, and giving them the distinctive title of the Scriptures, as different from all other writings. As the apostles and evangelists of our Lord, we always fully recognized their divine origin and quoted and wrote and preached from them appealing to them as authority on all questions of faith. We ever declared they were the 'Oracles of God,' and given as the Holy Ghost spoke by the mouth of His ancient servants. This is expressly declared of David, of Isaiah, and of all the holy prophets."

Peter now spoke and said, "You will remember in one of my epistles I spoke of our Lord's transfiguration on the holy mount and the voice that then spoke from heaven attesting that this Jesus was the Son of God. (2 Peter 1:17-21) Our combined testimony should have been received by every Jew. Yet, I then declared that the Scriptures were to them a more sure word of prophecy, and urged them to take heed to their revelations, for they fully spoke of Christ our Lord.

"Now," continued Peter, "there are the positive assertions of inspiration and authority for all the writings of the New Testament. What the four evangelists wrote was under the eye and inspection of our Lord, although not coming to public notice for years after His ascension to heaven. A special promise of the presence and help of the Holy Spirit was given to all the apostles. The Spirit of Truth thus promised was to bring to our remembrance whatever the Lord had taught us, and to teach us all things. Old truths brought back to mind, and new truths brought forth from the fountains above, were His special delight. On account of this endowment, our Lord placed an authority on our word as upon His own and the earlier prophets'. The writers of the New Testament always identify their words as the words of the Holy Ghost, announcing their messages as in truth the word of God: the word of the Lord that should endure forever. So from God they all came. They breathe the pure spirit of His goodness and carry the stamp of His authority, and will stand forever."

"Well," said Bohemond and I at the same time, "we would very much like to have a brief statement or summary of their teachings as you understand them now, for we would like to compare our own ideas of theology, and also that which is now taught in the churches, with the truth as it is."

They all assented quickly, and Abraham spoke, saying, "We will hand you such a statement shortly. In the meantime, if you care, you can take a flying trip in one of the passing chariots to a praise service on Broadway, or visit the park adjoining the Throne."

We thanked them for their friendly service and as we stepped on board a chariot, they said, "We will see you again soon," and waved us a pleasant good-bye. Isaiah kindly offered his services to go with us. We thanked him and the chariot soon slowed down at an entrance where thousands were gathering.

The place seemed to contain a space somewhat equal to a ten or twelve acre field in the earth. Circular rows of seats ran the whole course round the spacious place of worship. The orchestra occupied an elevated position in the center, and a thousand harps and voices were thrilling the vast audiences with the melodies of heaven. David's harp and voice never seemed so sweet as at that service. Many fathers of the church of an early date were there; many who had suffered persecution and martyrdom were also there. Their faces glowed with a peculiar joy as their words fell like fragrant oil upon that wonderful assembly. At the suggestion of St. Bartholomew we all fell on our knees and faces and with one heart and voice gave God all the glory. Many short sermonettes were preached to the thousands, many of whom like ourselves were newcomers into the city. This seemed to be a preparatory service for the great coming convocation at the Throne. Isaiah, with his long flowing beard, spoke as with a silver trumpet, announcing the general order newly arranged for the great occasion. Enoch's face shone equal to the angels' as he shouted the glory of his Lord. John the Baptist also with his piercing voice stirred the congregation as to a flame of fire. The blessed Virgin was also there and her sweet voice was like waves of light over all the people. We found she was held in great esteem in heaven. Priscilla and Aquilla both gave public utterances of great helpfulness. Many others witnessed to the great goodness of God. At last we all stood and sang a doxology and with one voice and as one soul shouted the praises of Him who had redeemed us to God by His own blood.

The services now closed and in leaving we saw many new arrivals from the earth, some were our own acquaintances. Oh, what joy in meeting these and to think we could now help them in their knowledge of the heavenly kingdom. They were so full of adoring wonder and praise that they could not restrain their feelings. In fact, we all felt much the same. We could not feel otherwise being in the very midst of the glory of God and in His blessed image, and in a reunion of long expectation with those of earlier years. We walked to a quiet place beneath the wide-spreading branches of a most lovely tree whose fruits were thickly hanging within easy reach and ripening every month. The fruit and leaves sent forth their fragrance delightfully and we all felt so enraptured by the presence and glory of God and the great provisions His love had planned for us, that I quickly suggested we all bow and give Him our heartfelt gratitude. We were all on our faces in a moment and it seemed our friends could never cease in saying, "Hallelujah to God." I at last said, "Would you like to go back to your earth home again and leave your mansions here?"

"Oh," said one of my dear old friends as he arose and grabbed my hand, "don't ask me such a question. That was only the cradle of our existence. This is our home. Oh, blessed be the Lord!"

We now gathered some fruit and communed together a long time. They told us of much of the doings of the communities we had left. I seemed to be back again, for the time being, among their homes, at their tables, driving with them along the roads and the streets, while they were speaking to me of these things. I said, "Oh, Scandinavia, my people by adoption, could I only see you all here and out of all your spiritual bondage and tradition, then would I shout the praises of God greater than ever."

I then said, "If they could only know that you have brought us this news when they were lowering your cold body into the grave, if they could only see you here in all this glory, and us having this precious visit beneath these majestic trees of life, then they would lift their eyes on high and say: 'Oh, that they had the wings of a dove, then would I fly away and be at rest.' (Psalm 55:6) Then with the anointed vision like the martyred Stephen of old, they might see heaven opened and the glories which the Son of God has prepared for all His children. (Acts 7:56) If their eye of faith could only penetrate the veil that hides the future—if they only could, with spiritual vision, but behold these glories—if they could only hear even the echo of the melodies which we have just heard, and of which Paul caught the tune of when transported to the third heaven, they would evermore say: 'For me to die is gain.' (Philippians 1:21)

The privileges of Christ in them by the Holy Ghost would mean much more to them than they do now."

Bohemond now said, "You have unbounded liberties here. Pluck from any of the trees as often as you like, go where you wish, enjoy everything you see. All are yours and you are Christ's and Christ is God's. We have found it wise not to hurry. You need be in no hurry. Eternity is before you."

So saying, we said good-bye, adding, "We will no doubt often meet again. We have an appointment near the Throne and will need to go to it. Later, we hope to meet you at the great convocations at the Throne itself. We will be greatly delighted to see you then."

We stepped on a chariot and were soon far out of sight or hearing of our friends. The light of the Throne greatly increased, and we stepped off just to meet our elder brethren whom we left some time since.

They now handed us the scroll which they had prepared, saying, "Study carefully and compare yourselves with it."

We thanked them for their great kindness and said a pleasant good-bye to them, also saying, "We hope to see you again soon at the Throne."

"Oh, yes, indeed," said Abraham. "We will be there, for it is of too important a character to be missed."

We now turned our faces toward a beautiful grove of shrubbery, many of the trees growing in a kind of circular form with the branches drooping all about, somewhat like the weeping willow of earth. When we came near, we saw two angels in most lovely apparel, sitting in the midst, on lovely upholstery. They arose and welcomed us and laying their hands on our heads, said, "We greet you in the name of our God. But what is that in your hand?"

"A scroll given us by the elders."

"Welcome to this grove and to these seats. The fragrance of these leaves will impart to you enlightening grace as you read and study." We sat down to wonder, but the angels had disappeared.

"We read and reread the sacred scroll, and rejoiced exceedingly to know that we felt in sweet harmony with the clear statements of divine truth contained in the document.

Bohemond now said, "Would to God my Bohemian brethren throughout the Austrian empire and elsewhere might only have the privilege of reading what the elders have written us."

"I was just thinking quite the same thing myself—that if the Scandinavian people as well as thousands of the churches in America and England could only study this orthodox code of divine doctrine, it might correct some of the modem errors and perversions of the faith, crept in among the people, through unfounded criticism of recent years. We must preserve this scroll, for it has been prepared with great care."

We now arose and took a long stroll among beautiful flowering shrubbery and gathered such fruit as we needed. We left this quiet seclusion and joined the multitudes on their way to the Throne. We had not gone far until many of the passing saints inquired concerning the scroll. We read it to them aloud and discussed its various doctrinal features to the great appreciation of everyone.

Just at this time there came a chariot filled with ancient men, whom we had not met before. They were driving very leisurely along. Their chariot seemed more like the Tally-Ho or a massive automobile of an earthly pattern. Seeing we were strangers, they at once invited us to ride with them. We accepted their invitation and the visit and the scenes which followed can never be fully described. °

CHAPTER TEN
The Elders' Scroll

This is the content of the Elders' scroll.

1. There is but one living and true God.

His Attributes

2. The attributes of God are the qualities, elements and perfections which belong to Him. They belong to Him and are parts of His divine nature— not that His whole being consists of a combination of them, but because they are the forms and expressions of His being which He has revealed to man.

3. These attributes are natural and moral. The natural attributes reveal His existence as an infinite and rational spirit; that is self-existence, freedom, omnipotence, omnipresence, omniscience, wisdom. The moral attributes are holiness, righteousness, justice, goodness, love, grace, mercy and truth.

4. As known to men on earth God is an invisible spirit, whom no man has seen nor can see. He is eternal and self-existent. He creates beings with immortality, but God alone possesses eternity. He is infinite, filling all space in the entire universe, embracing all worlds. He is omnipresent, i.e., infinite in power, shown by all His creations from the infinitely great to the infinitely small. All His acts are done by the exercise of His volition, and are seen

by man in the universality, variety and multitude of His works. God's omnipotence is limited only by His moral perfections. God cannot lie nor do any bad act, although He has the power.

5. God is omnipresent. The creator, upholder, and governor of all things. He is also omniscient, all things being open and naked before His eyes. God's wisdom is infinite, embracing all knowledge and is independent of all His creatures. We can tell Him nothing which He does not know, but His intelligent, infinite intuition comprehends all things past, present or future. This intelligence is perfect and absolute. Man analyzes things to find out their nature. God knows the nature without the analysis.

6. The foreknowledge of God is also absolute. How the foreknowledge of God is to be reconciled with man's free agency and moral accountability is indeed to men in the world a dark problem, but in the Scriptures both are clearly taught, and faith accepts what reason cannot reconcile. Some of the churches on earth have denied man's moral freedom. Others maintain that God in the exercise of His omniscience, like His omnipotence, abstains from knowing what His creatures will do under certain given circumstances. But the foreknowledge of God itself, unrevealed to men, does not impose nor even hint to me any course of behavior whatever; it in no degree affects his liberty of action. Man neither sins nor follows holiness, as the result of God's foreknowledge; so notwithstanding God's foreknowledge, He has made man in His image, a free moral being.

7. God is infinitely wise, always knows what is best, always adopts means which will best accomplish His purposes. That is wisdom, for wisdom is the art of turning our knowledge to best account. God's wisdom is seen in both creation and providence. His wisdom and His works everywhere confirm each other as being of God. No higher wisdom has ever been seen or known than God's wisdom in the plan of human redemption. It solves the problem of God's justice in justifying the believer in Jesus Christ.

8. The perfect goodness of God is seen in the benevolence which embraces all mankind and provides for their welfare. His merciful dealings with men declare His goodness. It is also seen in His unmerited favor, drawing man to salvation and in the use of so many means to this end also in the abundant provision which He has made for man's present and eternal happiness.

Moral Evil

9. How sin can exist in the world with all its terrible consequences in connection with God's righteous government is an awful and difficult problem, the complete solution of which is not possible to man in his earthly life. But sin does exist, and God permits it for reasons of His own, not fully revealed to men. In heaven it could not be so. No taint of sin can ever enter the gates of this city. If an angel should again sin God would instantly cast him down to hell.

10. Righteousness and justice are divine perfections. It is holiness exhibited in government. Truth or faithfulness of God is much the same as His righteousness. All He says and does is true. His truthfulness is an element of His character. God cannot lie. As God is eternal His truth remains the same. Whatever is out of harmony with His revealed truth, that is a lie. To the question, "What is truth?" this answer which we repeat in heaven is true, "To know God as He has revealed Himself to man is truth of the highest order." Our Lord declared: "I am the way, the truth and the life." All things taught or believed that are out of harmony with His clear revelations are both false and misleading.

The Triune God

11. The eternal God has revealed Himself to men as Father, Son and Holy Ghost. The Son of God is and always was divine. He is the express image of the Father. There have been many errors and heresies in the church in past ages. But we worship one Triune God neither confounding the persons, nor dividing the substances of them. For there is one person of the Father, another of the Son, and another of the Holy Ghost—but the Godhead of the Father, Son and Holy Ghost is one God.

The Divinity of Jesus Christ

12. He was the word of God from eternity. In the beginning
was the word and the word was with God, and the word was
God. While on earth we always held Him to be divine and
worshipped Him as God, and in heaven He is confessed by all,
both saints and angels, to be God and equal to the Father. All the
hosts of heaven worship Him. He was God manifest in the flesh.

The Holy Spirit

13. The Holy Ghost is one with the Father and with the Son—
equal in eternity, power and glory. In creation He moved upon
the face of the waters and developed form and beauty out of
disorder and confusion. He proceeded from the Father and from
the Son, and took up His abode with His church on earth. He has
been with them ever since His coming on Pentecost. He is the
comforter, guide and sanctifier of His people.

Man's Original State and Fall

14. God made man upright. He was both material and
spiritual and possessed of a divine life, and made in the image
of God. He could hold communion with God, with all that is
divine, as well as with the material universe. He was made but
a little lower than the angels, and was crowned with glory and
honor and had dominion over the works of God's hands in the
earth. He was a companion of his Father and Creator, capable of
admiring, adoring and enjoying God. While he was material and
possessed an animal nature, as he came from the hands of God,
yet he was an intellectual, moral, pure and holy being. He was
placed under law with life and death before him. Adam rebelled;
sin was born on earth. The glory of the Lord departed from him.
Man fell, and felt his guilt and was alienated from God. The
stream of humanity was contaminated at its source. The first
pair became sinful. Their descendants of necessity were in their
image fallen and depraved. So by one man sin entered into the
world and death by sin, and so death passed upon all men, for
that all have sinned. Our nature sinned in Adam and the stream
became polluted at the fountain head. This depravity became

universal for all the faculties and powers of the soul and body were brought under the power of evil.

The Atonement

15. We universally believe that the death of Christ was vicarious and propitiatory and that by it divine justice is satisfied, and God can be just and the justifier of all who believe in Christ Jesus, and that pardon and salvation is freely offered to all men, upon repentance and faith.

Election and Foreordination

16. We believe God did foreordain and devise a plan from the foundation of the world by which He would save man, and further, He did foreordain from the beginning, all men throughout the ages who would accept and be willing to conform to this plan, should be saved, so that everyone in harmony with His power and liberty of choice who shall choose eternal life though God's plan was foreordained to eternal salvation.

Repentance

17. True repentance is a condition of soul before God brought about by the operations of the Spirit of God upon the heart and soul of man whereby he is made to see and feel the sinfulness of his sins, and also to forsake them utterly and with full purpose of heart to yield obedience to God in the future.

Justification

18. Justification can only follow true repentance and is an act of God's free grace wherein He pardons the sins of man, and accepts him as righteous in His sight, only for the sake of Christ.

Faith

19. True unfeigned faith in God believes all that God has said, commanded, promised or threatened. It is dependent upon testimony, and is valuable to us as the truth itself. We can believe in men. We are responsible for our faith, for one may believe a lie as he does the truth. The truth only can make him free. True

saving faith leads the soul to trust itself to the all-atoning merits of the sacrificial death and resurrection of Jesus Christ.

Adoption

20. Adoption is an act of God whereby the believing sinner is received into the family of God, with all the rights and privileges of His children in which he becomes an heir of God with a right and title to eternal life.

The New Birth

21. The new birth of which our Lord spoke is that mighty change made by God in the soul of man when He imparts to him eternal life and renews him in the image of God. This change is the work of the Holy Spirit brought about in man, convincing him of sin, and leading him to repentance and faith whereby he is born from above with eternal life as a gift from God. P

*　　*　　*

Bohemond and I had just taken our seats in the chariot of the ancients. On inquiry we soon found we were in the chariot and the company of the earliest generations of the earth's population. We were soon introduced to Adam and Eve, the first parents of the chosen race. It seemed a little strange for us to think we were side by side with those of such early date. Abel, Enoch and Methuselah were also in the chariot. Turning to Abel, I addressed him and said, "Oh, you first-born son, born of those who never were born!"

"True," said Adam, who overheard the conversation, "we never were born, but created. I remember so distinctly when I first opened my eyes to behold the creations around me. I knew nothing, absolutely nothing at all. I felt the breezes and saw the waving of the branches of the trees and heard the sweet voice of birds and the lowing of cattle. God spoke intelligently to me about the fruit of the trees for food. I quickly learned how to satisfy my hunger and thirst. But I so very much wanted a mate, for I found none among all the creations of the garden. God gave me this woman as a helpmeet for me, so I found she was: 'bone of my bone and flesh of my flesh,' and I have loved her ever since."

At this Eve blushingly smiled and said, "You can guess our courtship was brief. It was me or none. But we soon learned life's lessons too, which all the world has repeated after us."

Seth and Noah were also side by side; Sarah and Rebecca, Keturah and Rachel also were grouped together; Ephraim and Manasseh must have seemed as young as when Jacob blessed them so long ago. Samuel and Aaron were also with the happy group and seemed to be rather presiding as prophet and priest over the chariot load. Caleb and Joshua were in the front assisting the charioteer in guiding the chariot. They all seemed to take a deep interest in us and asked us many questions bearing on modem times. After we had exchanged many questions both of modern and ancient life, I was so enraptured with the idea of eternal life, God's great gift to man, that I practically shouted and said, "Oh, what did God mean when He breathed into man the breath of life and man became a living soul? (Genesis 2:7) Here is the explanation before me in you dear brethren, who have survived the ravages of earth and the durations of heaven and are no older than you were four thousand or five thousand years ago. Oh, blessed eternal life!"

Bohemond now spoke and said to Methuselah, "Do tell me if your years on earth were as long as is stated in God's Book—nine hundred and sixty-nine years is the Bible record of your age. It seems to us almost unbelievable, as we only live such a short time now. Please tell us about it and what did you do?"

"Truly," replied Methuselah, "we lived to a great age and the record of the inspired word is correct, for Moses has told me repeatedly what he wrote concerning the early history of the world and man. As to why we lived so long, may be easily explained: God was exceedingly good to us. No former generations having lived before us, we had no books to read nor anything previously discovered by anyone before us. We had to find out by long searching and experimenting, which required years, which in a later day one could know in a few minutes. In fact, a child of only a few years, at a later period of the world, would know as much as one of us could kn hundred years had passed. After all the long years of our effort we all died (except Enoch over there), and after eight hundred or nine hundred years with but little more knowledge on general lines than your children of ten or twelve years know now. In the generations of men a little later, they would live as much in seventy-five or a hundred years as we would in eight hundred or nine hundred years. So God mercifully lengthened our lives and gave us greater opportunities to achieve the purpose which we were placed upon the earth, for our first habitation, instead of here in this celestial world. As to what we did, well, sure enough we did nothing but till the ground and herd the cattle and sheep. Our tools were indeed of the crudest sort and we made them wholly of wood. We did the best we could. Over there sits Adam; he can tell you, dear brethren (for so you are to us), all about his early experience."

At that I arose in the chariot and was introduced again to the venerable head of the race of man, and to Eve, the mother of us all.

"Oh, Adam and Eve, tell us of your early experience in the world."

"Certainly," said Adam, "with pleasure," and Eve made a lovely bow of assent.

"Well to begin: The garden where we were first placed was a lovely home indeed. No grander place could ever be found upon the earth. I have had descriptions of all kinds of earthly gardens, but nothing equaled paradise. Everything was perfectly delightful. Fruits of all kinds were ripening and hanging ready to our hand. Nothing forbidden to us but one tree. But, oh, that sin I never can forget it! What penalties followed our disobedience! The shame, disgrace and alienation from God!

"It was a sad day when God sent us out to till the ground and dig for ourselves. After we heard our sentence, we were very reluctant to leave, so there came two of the angels with whips in their hands and without discussion they drove us out. Oh, the sorrow and tears of that day! The angels had already told us of the tree of life, and its marvelous imparting virtues. The whole garden was charged and filled with the aroma of this tree. The very breezes and atmosphere were surcharged with life, but death was creeping upon us. We felt the chill and gloom of a terrible blow. We were simply out of harmony with our environments. The curse of death was upon us, and God sent us out to till the ground which He had likewise cursed."

"Did not God show you mercy and kindness and give the promise of a Redeemer for you?"

"Surely, He did, and gave us proofs of His love toward us in the garments He gave us to cover our shame."

"Did this signify anything to you then as an offering made by blood for sin?"

"Indeed, it did," said Adam, "for God fully explained to us the conditions of pardon. This we taught to our children and Cain knew it full well as did Abel, but Cain did not believe the details concerning the sin offering and this will explain to you why Abel brought a better sacrifice than Cain and by it though dead, yet he speaks."

"How was it, Abel?" I said.

"Just as father has told you," replied Abel.

"What about Cain?" I asked.

"He was self-willed and despised God's way. Poor boy, he sowed his seeds of unbelief and reaped his harvest among the lost."

"Will you tell me more about the results of your early sin when God drove you from the garden?"

"A thousand times I have told the story, but will cheerfully tell it again to you. Little did I comprehend before our sin the great depth and meaning of transgression. I know all that Moses wrote concerning it, and much beside, and his words were true; so also were the words of the Apostle Paul, all of which I know, for they have been repeated to me many times over. We had unbounded liberties in the garden and should have been content, but there stood the tree of knowledge very near the tree of life. God has said, 'Of every tree you may freely eat except one.' He threatened us with death should we disobey. Why we did disobey has been the awful problem of our lives. God let the penalty fall upon us. We became mortal and subject to death. The grant of immortality was withdrawn. We were depraved, and alienated from God. We lost His image and were without hope and without God. Only through His infinite mercy were we saved, and have the privilege of these mansions of bliss."

I thanked Adam and the rest for their kindness to us and said, "We hope we can have another such chance to talk like this with you."

"Oh, yes, we will be pleased at any time suitable to your convenience."

We now looked up the broad avenue in the direction we were going only to see it simply crowded with saints and angels bound for the great convocation at the Throne. These were in chariots of various descriptions, or walking leisurely along, eagerly engaged in joyful conversation and pleasant visits by the way. It reminded me of those great occasions in the world when ancient Israel was gathering at her great annual feast of the Lord at Jerusalem when a half million or a million souls would be gathering from cities, towns, and country throughout the Holy Land. But at this feast innumerable crowds were pouring in from all directions, those who had been gathered from all kingdoms, nations, tongues, kindreds and people of the earth, Israelites and Gentiles. No such gatherings have ever met in the world for any purpose as was gathering here.

But this time we were so near the Throne that great waves of light and glory were flashing out in all directions. An earthly sunrise on a bright June morning is but a faint picture of this glory. We were still many tens of kilometers[12] away, but the magnificent buildings and exquisite mansions were simply beyond description.

On both sides of this great avenue were the beautiful mansions built in the early days of heaven itself, which were in those early times occupied by the first saints who crossed the threshold of time into eternity. For there was a period in eternity when no soul of man walked these golden streets, nor saw, nor enjoyed this celestial glory, but from the days of Abel they began to gather here with an ever-increasing ratio. I was reminded again and again of our Lord's word on earth: "In my Father's house are many mansions," and truly, they had all been prepared

---

12. "Several leagues." That is a few miles, maybe 40. A league being about 5.7 kilometres (3.5 miles).

by our blessed Lord Himself, using angels and men as His helpers.

There were also very large and spacious mansions more especially for the angels, as I was told, where they congregate and worship God and where they receive the divine commandments and from which they often start on their missions of love to the world of sin and sorrow.

Lovely fountains were gushing up their silvery streams of life, in the midst of the streets, and with the golden vessels of this holy sanctuary we were constantly refreshing ourselves, for the chariot was moving very slowly and leisurely along.

Enoch now said, "We are almost at the southern entrance," and with this signal we all arose in the chariot and stood to our feet. The newer arrivals were so overcome and overawed by the majesty and glory of our surroundings that we began a hymn of praise. When we had finished the hymn, we all knelt upon the seats of the chariot and poured forth our praise to God. Bohemond shouted and said, "Oh, Throne of God, I am simply lost in the glory!"

Just at this moment David's chariot drove by our side. It was filled mostly with strangers, but among them was Genevive, my mother, and Mary. David had returned by the way of the cathedral and found room for them. Now both chariots stood still, and we all got out, and walked but a short distance and stood beneath the wide-spreading branches of one of the trees of life. Here we sang another hymn and again we fell on our faces with adoring praise. We were so overcome with the majesty and glory all around us that we knew not what to say or even think. Thousands of the saints were gathering about us and pressing on nearer the Throne. All those ancient men and women of the chariot went forward at once. But Bohemond, Genevive, mother, Mary and myself stood a few moments to consult further with each other and with David who now came to us.

With Bohemond and myself there was a fear and an awe we could not overcome. All the rest were perfectly at home, and we tried to be, but felt a shrinking in our souls. The thought of soon standing beside the Throne and looking in the face of the Great Jehovah made us think deeply of our preparation.

David now said, "Let us go on and join the countless multitudes over there."

Genevive and mother said, "If we are separated during this great service, we will meet you again at the banquet following." [q]

CHAPTER ELEVEN
The Splendors of the Throne

eyond all my power of description are the splendors of the Throne itself.

As we approached nearer the center of the great city and to the region of the Father's Throne, mighty waves of light and glory came constantly rolling over us, and with them came such refreshing baths of love, peace and joy, that our gladness was indescribable, having reached a degree of perfection never known before. The noiseless chariots were moving in all directions. Countless crowds of happy spirits, clothed in the purest garments and the expression of every face being that of the serenest peace and composure of soul were moving toward and away from the Throne.

Vast numbers like ourselves were approaching the Throne for the first time, many of whom had been within the boundaries of the majestic wall a long time, but the entire satisfaction with all the surroundings and the perfect contentment of soul made them linger long at each new object with which they came in contact. It was well for them that they did, for the glory of the Throne which excels all else would be too great for them.

I saw many who, on account of the majesty, glory and light, were so overcome, that it reminded me much of the experience of many on earth during great revival meetings, whose spiritual perceptions were greater than their physical ability to endure, so people would fall face down on the ground, or there would be trances, fainting, shoutings and kindred or shared spiritual experiences. I found even in heaven that there was a development and growth of the powers of the soul even to an endless perfection, and a strength of mental capacity unknown on earth or even at the first entrance into the heavenly state.

Yes, endless advancement, and still, while approaching, never quite able to reach the perfection of God.

The majesty of the Throne is indeed beyond description. Notwithstanding we had been graciously prepared for it, yet we were so overawed at our surroundings and the sight before us that we did not know what to say—or even think. Comparisons with earthly scenes, the richest and grandest or the greatest works of man would give but a faint idea—even human language itself is too tame to tell the story. The memories of childhood experiences were constantly rushing through our minds, so that I said to myself again and again, 'Is this only a dream or is it real? Have I seen a vision or am I really in heaven? No dream ever came to me on earth like this; no grandeur ever equaled it; no dream of glory so enchanting.'

We had been standing awestruck a long time, when a man whose face was beaming with a halo of light came to us; he seemed to realize our situation and said, "Dear brethren, have you just come to the Throne for the first time?"

As he came near us and spoke, we thought we recognized him, but having met so many in such a short time we were not sure that he was of those in the chariot. "Indeed," I replied, "we have been for quite a little time inside the city, but have been detained with so many things and wonderful scenes, that we could not reach the Throne earlier."

"You have been wise," said our friend, who was interesting himself in us, "for even now you are none too well prepared for the great things which are just before you. If you would like to have me, I will accompany you for just a little while in your introduction to this most blessed and exalted place in our Father's house."

"We would be much pleased to have you do so, for we don't understand much of what is before us." I turned to Bohemond and said, "How fortunate to have such company and assistance, and yet we knew that in our Father's house with its many mansions we need have no fears for our needs would be met at the right time."

At this he brought us to a sparkling fountain not far from one of the great entrances to the Throne, and with a golden goblet gave us a drink, then he went a little distance to a mammoth tree whose branches were everywhere hanging low and brought us each a cluster of its fruit, when we had eaten it, he pronounced a blessing upon us and suddenly our eyes and minds were prepared for the greatest glories to which a mortal man has ever been exalted, and to those scenes we will now turn our attention.

*　　*　　*

We were so entranced at the vision before us that Bohemond fell on his face and poured forth his praise to God as I had never heard him before. In fact, we all felt completely overcome in wonder and admiration.

The vastness of the various compartments of the Throne is beyond all earthly comparison. For several kilometers[13] it was spread out in all directions before us. Bohemond came close to my side and said in a low voice, "Whoever could have thought of such glory!" Light, all filled with glory, heightened beyond all human conception of earthly things revealed the splendors of the Throne beyond the powers of a man to describe, so that I kept thinking of the word which I had so long heard: "That God is light and in Him is no darkness at all." (1 John 1:5) We stood long in wonder and admiration.

Our guide now came to us and said, "We will now go forward and see more of the greatness of this, our Father's Throne. You need have no fears, for we are all children of God and He delights in our highest enjoyment and is pleased for us to know of these treasures of His love. So come with me, and I will show you at a glance a little of what God had in mind when He laid the foundations of the earth and made man in His own image.

---

13. "Many furlongs." That is a few miles. One furlong being about 200 meters (660 feet).

"I have been here during thousands of earthly years. There were but few of earth's inhabitants when first I came, compared to the unnumbered millions now, but a vast number of angels were about the Throne when first I looked upon this glory."

"Yes," I said to him, "and I remember in God's word it is said: 'Ten thousand times ten thousand angels are about the Throne.'"

"Sure," said Bohemond, "and that is a hundred million and I think there is room for a hundred million more!"

We found that our guide was none other than Enoch of ancient birth, whom we had met in the chariot and also at our first entrance into paradise and again at one of the great praise services in this city. But we had met so many hundreds and even thousands in such a short time and then the bewilderment that came over us at the great sight, we were slow in distinguishing him from so many ancient men. His body shone like the light itself and he was the picture of health and youth and the man of all others, who never tasted death. "Oh, Enoch, you blessed of God!"

"Come with me," said he, and we followed him to a raised elevation many feet above the floor of the Throne. From this we could see the innumerable company which John saw in his vision, or such portion of it as our eyes could reach, which no man could number. Countless crowds from all nations of earth clothed in the purest white garments. They seemed to be moving in all directions in a joyous service for their Lord.

I said in a subdued voice to Bohemond, "I wonder if John is anywhere among this mighty host, for I do remember his words how he foretold this wonderful scene: 'After this I beheld and lo, a great multitude which no man could number of all nations and kindreds and peoples and tongues stood before the Throne and before the Lamb, clothed with white robes and palms in their hands.'" (Revelation 7:9)

Enoch now said, "Shall we now go further on, for there are wonderful scenes yet before you!"

"Oh, indeed, we should like to see all."

"But," said Enoch, "you will be here a long time before you see all."

As we passed along, we again met many whom we had seen in other parts of the city. Everyone seemed so contented and happy. They wanted nothing they did not have. There were differences in the experiences of the people, but the holy harmony was like the music of the strings of a harp—not a discord throughout the entire realm of the city or even paradise.

Enoch now led us to the Throne itself. It was encircled by wonderful majestic bands of light with all the colors of the rainbow, which signified the attributes of the Almighty God and Father of us all. We seemed now to comprehend God as we never had before. I thought of the band of light that encircles the planet Saturn, the gold tinged clouds of an earthly sunset, but no comparison could describe its glory. Beneath the circle of this rainbow was the seat of the Almighty Father. For beauty, grandeur, glory and majesty, it cannot be described. It was simply upholstered glory, with all the colors of the rainbow tinting everything.

Now it will not do to think of the Almighty in His greatness and power as consisting in bulk. Every attribute of the Father was in His Son, Jesus Christ. All power was His, both in heaven and earth, and while He is everywhere present at the same time, yet His omnipresence does suggest that He is a person and that person has a seat on His Throne and from this Throne issues the governing power of the universe. His spirit and power are operating in all worlds and His Throne is likewise in all celestial kingdoms.

"Had you not been prepared for it," said Enoch, "you could not have endured this exceeding glory."

Just at this moment Moses, whom we had met at one of the fountains near the Judean gate and with whom we had such a pleasant visit, now stepped to our side, and with a pleasant bow of recognition he said, "Dear brethren, be not overawed with this glory, nor with the fear to see your Father's face, for you are in His image now. I once wished and prayed on earth to see His face—yet I did not really know what I was asking for. God declared to me then that no man could see His face and live, yet He veiled His face while His glory passed before me, but I did see His back parts—but now you can look upon His face and not only live, but enjoy the vision with increasing raptures throughout eternity."

"Oh, bless His name!" I said. "My soul is so filled with exceeding joy at the inexpressible glory of this scene, that I cannot restrain my feelings," so with many others who were standing quite near us and who had recently come to the Throne, we fell before God with adoring praise and continued doing so for a long time. Suddenly we heard a mighty chorus of voices of ten thousand times ten thousand angels, along with the innumerable company of saints, saying, "Blessing and honor and glory and power be unto Him that sits on the Throne and unto the Lamb forever and ever."

As we arose I saw the glory of God as I never had before. His face was as the light and all His divine attributes seemed revealed and stood out in such sweet harmony that I could only think of love, goodness, mercy, power, wisdom and knowledge, and that all our needs would be supplied by Him.

I looked again, and such pure and holy thoughts filled all my soul. I thought of some lines I had learned long ago:

> Eternal light, eternal light
> How pure that soul must be
> When brought within thy searching sight,
> It shrinks not, but with calm delight,
> It lives and looks on you.
> His all-seeing eyes were eyes of love.

I knew that all things in heaven and earth and in all worlds both small and great were naked and open before these eyes. His hands, I knew, had made them all.

Enoch and Moses both stood close to us and said, "We have been here for thousands of earthly years and yet we only begin to know God. You may think you have seen those eyes, yet you have only seen one ray of light compared to what you will see. You may think you have seen His feet, yet the earth from which you have so recently come is only one small footstool."

"Oh, yes, indeed," I replied, "I just now remember His word: 'Heaven is my throne and earth is my footstool.'" (Isaiah 66:1, Acts 7:49)

"His greatness," said Moses, "you can never know. You see Him seated on His Throne, but then His Almighty Spirit is everywhere. His creative skill lacks no knowledge, and His everlasting energy knows no fatigue. He is never weary in upholding all His works. His all-hearing ear listens to all rightly offered prayers. His omniscient eye sees everything. His almighty hands are quick to bless or curse. His will simply becomes almighty law."

I looked again, to scan the Throne once more, and saw twenty-four seats of most exquisite beauty on both sides of the Throne. I knew from the blessed word these were for the elders (Revelation 4:4)—but they were mostly vacant now, for the elders, I had found, are very busily engaged in service for Him who is on this Throne—yes, the Throne of the universe. I saw further that the Throne consisted of a double compartment and I at first wondered. But Enoch came, seeing my perplexed curiosity, and said to us, "Our Lord Jesus who reigns both in heaven and on earth has likewise His seat on the Throne, with His Father, for He overcame and forever has His seat on this Throne."

I quickly remembered the scripture where in the Gospel it is declared, that: "He was received up into glory and sat on the right hand of God," (Mark 16:19) and again the blessed martyr Stephen said: "I see the heavens open and the Son of Man standing on the right hand of God."(Acts 7:56)

I said to Enoch, "Where is He now?"

"Oh, He is somewhere about the Throne, or in the city; you will see Him soon, for He is always at the great convocations at this place. Have you not met Him?"

"Yes, indeed, at the Judean gate, and at a great praise service in another part of the city, but I am eager to see Him again."

"You will be delighted with inexpressible joy beyond all you have yet met or seen, when not only Himself but the great convocation of saints and angels occurs, which will be quite soon. We often meet here for further explanations of the kingdom by our Lord or His servants, and of God's further purposes with His people. We have not yet learned all there is to know about the purposes and plans of God concerning these mighty multitudes of the saved."

"Those most honored of God as His servants on earth, are greatly honored here," said Enoch, "and are His ministers in heaven. These often take part in the elaborations of eternal truth. Of course, you will not leave the Throne until the great praise service is over?"

Bohemond came up and said, "Well, I do not think we will ever want to leave. I feel such glory in my soul. I never even dreamed while in my earthly life that such real things were in store for us."

Then I looked again into the face of Him who sits on the Throne and said, "Oh, my God, my Father, I praise You forever, for ever thinking of me, an unworthy mortal man, and for bringing me to this exceeding glory!"

"Now," said Enoch, "I must leave you for a time, for I see the mighty crowds are coming from all quarters of the city." And so saying he waved with his hand a most pleasant good-bye, as he said, "I will see you again." Moses also had disappeared among the millions of happy souls.

Bohemond and I now stood in wonder and with increasing praise to God for the great things we were now beholding when suddenly four mighty angels arose and were flying about the Throne, having golden trumpets in their hands, and with one great blast they made the arches and domes of heaven ring. But they quickly disappeared through the great avenues of the city. We knew the meaning and to what followed we will now turn our attention.

* * *

I turned and said to Bohemond, "What shall we do? I feel such an awe and fear, we know so little of the order of things here." We asked some standing near us about it.

"Oh," said they, "have no fears, go where you like—we will all find our places, and you will be near the Throne."

We widened the circle of our vision and behold, we saw a vast number of seats both at the back and also at the right and left of the Throne. They rose in terrace form like a great amphitheater. These, we soon found, were filling up with the great choir of heaven. They filed in with beautiful order, each having a golden harp. At last the seats were all filled with those who had been the most devoted leaders in the choirs of earth, with very many also who never sang in an earthly concert, but because of heavenly musical voices trained in the praises of God on earth, they were chosen by the blessed Bishop of all souls in heaven for these great occasions.

I looked again. The elders had mostly taken their places, many of whom we had met. They gave a lovely bow of welcome. When all our cares were met we felt much at home.

I looked again, with adoring wonder, and lo, our blessed Lord Jesus Himself accompanied by Moses and Paul came to the Throne. Our Lord took His place beside His Father & Moses and Paul beside the elders.

Countless crowds were pouring in from all directions. Chariots were bringing tens of thousands. The robes of the high priest of ancient times could not compare to the beautiful flowing draperies of these millions of the blood-washed. All seemed so happy and joyous. Many of our friends whom we had known on earth so well, and who had come from remote parts of the city or paradise now came to greet us. My own mother, Genevive and Mary were among them. Dear old grandfather, now so young and beautiful, also stood with us. Several comrades of my youth, who had passed on many years ago also came. Among them was one whom I never expected to see in heaven, but who, like the thief on the cross, was saved in the last days of his life, and although he had spent a long time in the remoter regions of paradise as he afterward told me, yet now he was here. We had many congratulations and joyful unions, while the great assembly was filing in.

For five or six kilometers[14] or more distant from our great Father's seat was the outer circle of the mighty crowd gathered

---

14. "Thirty furlongs." That is about 3.75 miles. One furlong being about 200 meters (660 feet).

beneath the great arched canopy of this imperial Throne. The four angels now returned and flying in the midst of the Throne, were sounding through their trumpets, saying, "Holy, holy, holy is the Lord God Almighty, which was, and which is, and which is to come." When those archangels had finished this note of praise, then the twenty-four elders fell down before Him that lives forever and ever, and sits on the Throne, and worshipped Him, saying, "Worthy are You our Lord and our God to receive the glory and the honor and the power for You did create all things and because of your will, they are and were created."

While they were lying prostrate on their faces, the great choir of one hundred thousand voices arose and sang a new song before the great company, which for sweetness, sentiment and feeling was never equaled on earth—not one discordant voice or harp was heard among them, but the music rolled up and away, and reached even with its faintest tones to those in the utmost limits of this wondrous gathering, for in the pure atmosphere of heaven voices can be heard for a long distance, and all the great assembly replied, "Amen and amen." I looked again, and behold, I saw ten thousand times ten thousand angels and heard them sing with loud voices saying, "Worthy is the Lamb that was slain to receive power and riches, and wisdom and might and honor and glory and blessing." And all the elders stood and said, "Amen."

They then announced a familiar hymn, familiar to earth as well as heaven, for I had heard it many years ago. The choir led, but all the people sang and praised God until I certainly thought that the earth itself would resound with these praises and echo back the wonderful melody. I was so entranced that an awe and fear again took hold of me as I saw the greatness and wonderfulness of Almighty God as I never had before.

I looked again and an elder whom I had met, invited to his side by gesturing with his hand. I quickly obeyed and jumped up to the great gallery where the elders sat, and he said, "Look again at the great crowd beyond," and I saw indeed the great multitude which no man could number, out of every nation and of all tribes and peoples and tongues standing before the Throne, and before the Lamb, dressed in white robes, having palms in their hands, and they shouted with one great voice, saying, "Salvation to our God which sits upon the Throne and unto the Lamb," and all the angels fell on their faces and worshipped God and said, "Amen."

After this, at the elder's suggestion, I descended to the floor of the Throne and joined the company I had left, and in a low voice I said, "I never knew how to worship God before. Our love and zeal were so cold in the earth, and our worship so formal and lifeless."

"Truly," whispered Bohemond. "If I only were back to earth for one single week I would teach my people how to worship God. It does seem a little strange that we loved God so little while on earth."

After this little episode of conversation had passed, our Lord arose and stood and with one motion of His hand, before His majestic presence, profound silence reigned, and every head was bowed before Him who was our All in All.

* * *

As our Lord arose to speak, all heads were deeply bowed for a few moments and then most earnest attention was given. We all hung on His words as when He spoke the sermon on the mount on earth. The theme was, "The coming dispensation, now about to be ushered in, when He shall once more descend to the earth taking with Him all this mighty assembly of saints and angels, when will occur the resurrection of the bodies of all His saints."

The great audience listened with profound attention and received the word with great gladness, for everyone was deeply interested personally in the matter. Thousands of saints shouted aloud with joy at the thought that so soon would occur the "redemption of the purchased possession."

The angels themselves were dancing for joy, for our Lord had said that they should take a most prominent part in the great event. Very many, indeed, of the unnumbered and countless host had been waiting for this even for thousands of years, and waiting for their spiritual bodies which we knew would be given us at that time. Then we should be equal to the angels themselves, which the elders now are, and are preferred before them, for the place of the elders indicated this, being near the Throne.

The emotion and feeling which our Lord displayed during this sermon was beyond anything we were accustomed to on earth. We were melted into deep emotion. He expounded at great length on the ideas which Paul had advanced so long ago while writing under divine inspiration when he said: "Having made known unto us the mystery of His will, according to His good pleasure which He has purposed in Himself: That in the dispensation of the fullness of time, He might gather together in one all things in Christ, both which are in heaven and which are on earth, even in Himself." He called attention to the superior advantage the elders now have on account of their resurrection. He described to the mighty host the order of events in connection with the closing history of His spiritual reign on earth, the events of the last times, the great political changes, and devastating wars of the closing period. He declared also that in the last times great effort would be made among the leading civilized nations to bring about a peaceful settlement of national troubles. That much had been done and much remained to be done.

How quickly I thought of the words of the prophets when he wrote concerning this same theme: "They shall beat their swords into plow shares and their spears into pruning hooks." (Isaiah 2:4)

He went on to speak of the worldly character of many of the churches on earth, their loss of spiritual power, and the very great slowness of making disciples of all nations, many of the churches having almost forgotten their real mission in bringing the world back to God, as He repeated again some of His words uttered so long ago: "The church is the salt of the earth, but if the salt has lost its savor wherewith shall it be salted?" (Matthew 5:13) As He spoke upon this point a holy fervor and deep emotion clothed His words until the mighty crowd most solemnly bowed their heads with the very impressive thought that His words had a deep meaning suited to many thousands of us only a little while ago.

Oh, how many of us whispered to ourselves and to those about us, "If I only could go back even for a brief time, how differently I would live and labor for the great end for which our Lord suffered and died."

He spoke also of the alarming formalities in so many of the Protestant and Catholic churches, of the corruptions and whoredoms so extensive throughout the world. As He was speaking of the degeneracy of His church on earth, I most deeply felt the force of His words uttered nearly two thousand years ago: "When the son of man shall come, will He find faith on the earth?" (Luke 18:8) "But," said He, "there is a very great crowd of blood-washed souls who are looking for His return and faithfully toiling while waiting for their adoption into this mighty company above." He hinted again that the time was drawing near when He, with all this great assembly, with millions in paradise and all parts of the celestial city, should again go back to celebrate the earth's great Sabbath.

Mighty angels with their trumpet voices should lead the hosts until the thousands of thousands of chariots should reduce their speed and slow to a stop in the regions of that terrestrial world. Then the great trump of God should be sounded, of which the blast of Sinai was but a little hint, and awaken all the dead saints who should instantly rise with spiritual bodies and each soul of us should have our own.

When He had thus spoken, all this mighty host led by the angels, shouted, "Hallelujah! the Lord omnipotent reigns!"

"And further," He said, "the living saints who have never died will never die. Death shall have no dominion over them, but from thenceforth is destroyed forever, and with them we shall be joined in one great united church, world without end." Again the great crowd said, "Hallelujah!"

But the most solemn and moving of all His utterances from the Throne before the great assembly was His reference to a present condition of the church on earth. He referred to a new and most cunning device of Satan, the old enemy of man, to introduce into the church of all Christendom a most destructive criticism of the Holy Scriptures. "This," He declared, "is a revelation of the man of sin—the son of perdition, only in a new form in the last days. The mystery of iniquity was at work in the early days of the church in the various forms of the spirit of anti-

Christ, but it was withheld until the Gentile world should have their opportunity of salvation. But now that wicked one is being revealed whose coming is after the working of Satan and with all deceivableness in them that perish because they received not the love of the truth that they might be saved. So they are denying much of the Holy Scriptures of God, nearly all the Old Testament saints and all that is miraculous, even assailing His own divine origin, miracles and atonement. And so God shall send them strong delusion that they should believe a lie (2 Thessalonians 2:11).

"Oh, Satan," he shouted, "your doom will soon be sealed in the vortex of hell."

I can only repeat a little of His sermon. When He closed, a number of the elders followed Him with brief elaborations of truth somewhat along the lines of which He had already spoken.

Many, like ourselves thought how clearly the blessed Book of God on earth has told us many of these things, and what comfort, as well as sorrow, to the saints to know the great things which are yet before us!

Far in the distance as our eyes could reach we saw the seats glittering like the purest gold, raised amphitheater-like, to a great elevation which entirely encircled the majestic Throne.

Many responsive hymns were sung, those in the distance responding with choruses, which seemed like great waves of the sea that rolled in splendor over the great crowds of the redeemed. At last, the great convocation was drawing toward its close. Our Lord now arose and with a voice distinctly heard to the utmost bounds of the Throne, invited us to a royal banquet given by Himself in honor of the most recent arrivals. The doxology of heaven was sung by the great crowd. Our Lord's benediction and dismissal followed. We all retired to a great pleasure ground just next to the Throne on the east. Many hundreds of rows of tables, about five kilometers[15] in length, were spread before us. These were loaded with the richest choice foods that paradise ever knew. A hundred varieties of the tree of life grow everywhere in the city, but especially in the valleys and upon the hillside of

---

15. "More than twenty-four furlongs." That is about three miles. One furlong being about 200 meters (660 feet).

paradise. Twelve kinds of fruit grow on each tree. From these the tables were most gorgeously furnished. The angels were waiters at the tables and surely we lacked for nothing.

As we were eating, Bohemond arose and said, "My brother, Seneca, look at what is before us." I arose and looked across the great sea of human spirits interspersed with many thousands of angels whose delight it was to serve these honored guests. Far toward the center of this great dining hall was a stupendous fountain, a fountain of fountains. It was indeed immense in its dimensions and the height of its spray. The royal gardens, fountains and palaces of the kings of the earth could in no wise be compared to it. From this fountain we were all refreshed and also from the river of life from which its multitude of branches have their source.

While eating and drinking with the saints of all ages, and in the presence of our King, we certainly thought of the words of the Book and how truly the beloved disciple had written concerning these great occasions: "And the Lamb which is in the midst of the Throne shall feed them and shall lead them unto living fountains of water, and God shall wipe away all tears from their eyes." (Revelation 7:17) 'Indeed,' I thought to myself, 'and who can ever cry again but those of the lost ones who shall lift up their eyes, being in torment?'

During the banquet the great choir sang many new and beautiful hymns of praise. While our Lord gave everyone such a glad welcome, and especially those who had so recently entered the doorways of paradise and passed through the gates of the city and were now forever at home. Many of the ancient men and women also took part in giving short words of welcome.

David also tuned his harp and sang the words of the beloved disciple in meter, which nearly everybody in heaven knows: "And God shall wipe away all tears from their eyes, and there shall be no more death, neither sorrow nor crying, neither shall there be any more pain, for the former things are passed away. And He that sat upon the Throne said, Behold I make all things new. And He said unto me write, for these words are true and faithful. I am Alpha and Omega, the beginning and the end. I will give unto him that is athirst, of the fountain of the water of life freely, and he that overcomes shall inherit all things and I will be his God and he shall be my son." (Revelation 21:4-7)

Again the congregation shouted, "Hallelujah," and the choir sang the dismissal.

We were now soon scattering for distant points of the city. A hundred thousand chariots were filled with the busy hosts of heaven. Salutations and momentary good-byes were heard everywhere. Smiling happy faces knew no limit to the joyful expressions and greetings with which every soul overflowed. Not one conflict or discord or ruffled feeling or disappointed look was to be seen anywhere. Oh, this was heaven indeed!

When the great crowd had somewhat disappeared, there still remained an innumerable company of saints and angels. The returning chariots were bringing multitudes of others in place of those who had gone. Those who led the music and sang their sweet solos had nearly all gone. The seats of the elders were vacant, but hosts of others were crowding in. As one of the elders passed near us, Bohemond and I called him to us for a conversation.

He said, "Let us step on a chariot and go to a quiet place." In a few moments we were slowing down at one of the fountains just outside one of the gateways to the Throne. After giving us a drink from the fountain, he said, "We will now walk to the cluster of trees over there." From them we gathered some fruit and sat down to have him explain the mystery to us. [s]

CHAPTER TWELVE
Visit with Daniel

The elder, which proved to be Daniel the prophet, and who was by our side, now said to us, "Well, dear brethren, I am glad to have this visit with you. I know you have recently arrived in the city and are eager to know of the wonders which are constantly crowding upon you."

He told us, "Jesus our Lord, who was conceived by the eternal spirit and born of the Virgin Mary, is Lord of earth and heaven. All power has been given to Him by His Father. While I was in the earth I knew Him long before His advent by the Virgin Mary, as the 'Ancient of Days,' whose garment was white as snow and the hair of His head like pure wool.

"In the revelations which God then gave me I saw Him 'sitting on His Throne in the last judgment and His Throne was like a fiery flame. A fiery stream, or bands of flaming angels, issued and came forth from before Him; a thousand thousand ministered to Him and ten thousand times ten thousand stood before Him; the judgment was set and the books were opened.'" (Daniel 7:9-10)

At this Bohemond clasped his hands and said, "Oh, Daniel, greatly beloved, I remember the part of Scripture which you have just quoted."

"Indeed," said the elder, "and it will stand as my testimony from God till the time of the end."

He continued, "Man has been created in the likeness and image of the Triune God. In his creation he was lower than the angels, but in his redemption and glorification he is their equal and in some respects their superior. All these great multitudes of the redeemed are the bride of our Lord and He is complete only in them, which is His fullness and very precious to Him. Have you not noticed how completely in His image we are?"

"Indeed," I replied, "and who could have believed when we were children playing in the dirt and dusk of the earth, that all this exaltation and glory was in store for us. We were taught about heaven, but how little we conceived of its glory and grandeur."

"Sure enough," said the elder, "you have seen but little of our Father's house and the many mansions it contains. Tell me where you have been. Maybe I can help you still further in the unfoldings and knowledge of this great Kingdom of God."

"Oh," said Bohemond, "we first met each other far down the river in a remote portion of paradise. We came from the earth about the same time and have been much together since we spent some time about the river and met several ancient men and learned our first lessons and hymns on the river banks.

"Abraham brought our company to the Judean gate, where we first met our Lord and received His smiles of welcome. We have visited the children's praise service at the Polytechnic and also a great praise meeting on Fourth Avenue. We also visited the Shrine of Sacred Relics, and have attended a most interesting convention of the prophets and apostles and writers of the Bible, called to discuss the condition of the church on earth, their doctrinal disputes and errors which have crept in among them from time to time, and many scenes of the deepest interest have met us at every turn since entering the city. Our souls have been constantly filled with wonder and admiration every moment of our time since leaving the earth in the angels' chariot."

"Well," said Daniel, "you have only seen the threshold of your inheritance when compared to the vastness and greatness of the provisions for you. But as to what is before you, eternity is short enough to show it all. But be assured that your enlarging cup of enjoyment will always be full. You have noticed how completely free you are from unrest and without aches or pains of any kind and that no distress or trouble burdens or haunts you here, such as we all experienced so much while in the earth, but these things are all passed away, and your appreciation of heaven is greatly increased by the bitter cups of your earthly life.

"You will have such important employment here as will make life the most meaningful. The occupation and business of your earthly life was but a preparation for and a little reflection of heaven. There is no toil here, like the sweat of our brow of which we used to know so much, but a joyful employment of all the powers of the soul to further the interest of all about us.

"Whatever you were most accustomed to do on earth will aid in your busy life in heaven. Were you in the agricultural departments of the earth, then you will often enjoy your visits to the plains, valleys, hills and mountains of paradise. These with their abounding fruitfulness and scenery will be of great delight to you and with the increasing multitudes gathering here from the earth, enlarged provisions are constantly being made for them in which you will delight to share.

"Have you been a teacher, then you will greatly enjoy the service of instructing those who have just come from terrestrial shores to this eternal kingdom. Those who were mechanics will find ample scope for that trait of mind in heaven. Our Lord has been preparing these mansions for us for thousands of years, but He employs the busy hands of millions of his saints in the most wonderful architecture of heaven.

"But now for you, dear brethren, all you see before you is for your enjoyment and comfort. The chariots are for your journeys. If you wish you can go at the speed of sound—go at your pleasure. Massive praise services of which we are all so fond here, are held in various sections of the city. If you wish to ascend to the higher or lower galleries or sections of the city, step into the elevator and press the number of the button and you may in a few moments be landed hundreds of kilometers[16] above or below as you desire. For you will remember that the city lies four

16. "A thousand furlongs." That is about 125 miles. One furlong being about 200 meters (660 feet).

square, its length and breadth, its height and depth are equal, being like a solid cube, twelve thousand furlongs each side."

"Oh, how massive and great is our inheritance!" said Bohemond. "Twelve thousand furlongs would be fifteen hundred miles of earthly measurement."[17]

"Sure enough," said the elder, "and there are nearly four hundred thousand of these sections or stories of the city, beside all the vast illimitable regions of paradise. A thousand years of an earthly count will have passed before you have seen but a small portion of what is yours forever. Its vastness is beyond your ability to comprehend at present. So you see, you have ample room for the growth and development of your inquisitive soul."

At this I clasped my hands and with great ecstatics of joy cried out, "Oh, Daniel, greatly beloved, is there no end to the provisions God has made for us?"

The elder replied, "The resources of heaven are inexhaustible, and as to the height and depth of the city, its length and breadth—you can never take it all in, but go where you will and you will find that the busy hosts of God know no fatigue and they will welcome you to any and all their banquets and feasts and services of song and praise as we have here.

"If you desire a trip to the beauties and scenery of any part of paradise, any one of the saints or angels will be glad to accompany you, for we all take pleasure in each other's comfort here. Let us now step to that raised section at the four corners near us." We climbed the spacious stairway. "Now will you look down this avenue toward the far distance over there?"

We did so, and as we stood above the busy crowds and countless hosts, all who were once children of earth, and who, like ourselves, once shared in the toils and sweat of an earthly life, and with us had struggled against the fearful hosts of sin, but now exalted and glorified with our blessed Redeemer, the elder said, "Are you repaid for your faith and service for your Lord in the world?"

"Repaid," I said, "what did I ever do to deserve this? No, no, it's all of grace. God is love. We were nothing; we did nothing but cling to Jesus. He was our All in All."

---

17. Or about 2,400 kilometers.

Visit with Daniel

"Will you now look to the north?" and he pointed with his finger the way, for we knew no north nor south, for no sun shone at noonday, nor any north star at midnight, for there is no noonday nor midnight in heaven. We needed not the light of sun, nor moon for the Lord God and the Lamb is our eternal light.

As we looked in the directions suggested, we saw the avenue was broad and lovely and the mansions were of exquisite beauty. The golden streets were as warm with so many happy people. Thousands of children were playing in the streets. Lovely fountains were throwing up their spray which sparkled like beaded diamonds of light. We saw long tables a half kilometer long[18] each most beautifully adorned and loaded with most precious fruits and nuts of all varieties, and with such freedom everyone seemed to be eating and drinking at his ease and pleasure.

I thought in what a different sense could all this mighty crowd say in the same words of many of the Jews of old: "We have eaten and drunk in your presence and You have taught in our streets." (Luke 13:26)

"Many of these children," said the elder, "have but recently come, but you see how completely contented they are. No change of place nor surroundings could make them happier, unless it would be to see their parents, brothers, sisters or friends here—then their cup of happiness would be complete indeed. They have no desire to go back to the earth from where they have so recently come, but they do greatly rejoice in the coming of their friends. Contentment of which we only knew the first basic idea of while in the world is written on every soul here.

"Will you now look upward," said the elder.

We looked above. To our greater wonder still, the arches and domes above us were ablaze with the sparkle of what seemed to be the most precious diamonds for beauty, and jasper stones clear as crystal.

This," said the elder, "is but a reflection of the glory of God which shines out from the Throne and through all His works."

---

18. "A thousand cubits." That is about 1,500 feet or 450 meters. A cubit is about 18 inches, or about half a meter.

"Now," said the elder, "I must leave you and bid you good-bye. The blessings of the eternal God are forever yours. Great things are in store for you, but I will see you again," and he disappeared among the countless crowd.

*　*　*

We stood a moment almost bewildered at the great scenes before us in every direction. We now descended from this great platform or elevation, to find David's chariot was standing nearby. Mother, Mary and Genevive had just stepped from it. Oh, indeed, it was a glad surprise to see them again in the midst of the great moving crowd about us. We held hands and with a love-kiss, clean and pure as heaven itself, we all felt that the unions begun on earth were far sweeter here than any family ever knew while in the earthly life in the flesh. But no wifehood nor husband's place is desired or hardly thought of in heaven.

David now said, "I must bid you good-bye. The visits and journeys with you have been most pleasant indeed, but I will see you all again. Gabriel with his chariot stands over there for you. Before you go, shall we not join in one more service of thanksgiving and praise?"

Bohemond practically shouted at this and we all took our harps and joined David in one more sweet hymn of praise. When we had finished, David waved his hand a pleasant farewell, and his chariot moved away and was lost from our gaze as we followed him with longing eyes, for we had learned to love him so very much.

Gabriel now came and addressed us most lovingly. Mother, Genevive and Mary all knew him well, but I had only seen him once since he said good-bye to me at my first entrance into paradise, but I found he was one of the chief angels of heaven, one of the archangels, yet he was Daniel's servant while yet in the world. I found he led the band who announced the birth of the Saviour and guarded the sepulcher at His death and rolled back the stone at His resurrection.

He now invited us to seats with him in the chariots. "For," said he, "I am sent into paradise." We accepted his invitation and were soon stepping into the first chariot of heaven, and one that has traversed the distance between heaven and earth multiplied thousands of times. In that chariot we were soon all seated.

The angel now said to mother and Genevive, "Have you any choice of routes for the journey through paradise? We have a command concerning Seneca, and you are more than welcome to journey with us to the gateway."

"Indeed," they both spoke at once, "we would be greatly pleased to go with you, and you may choose the route for you know best."

"Perhaps Seneca has a choice."

"Oh, Gabriel, you blessed of God, you choose for us, for you have knowledge of all places in the kingdom which we don't have."

"Leaving it to me then we will go by way of the mountain regions which lie to the southeast, going out at Benjamin's gate."

"Good," said Genevive, "nothing could please Mr. Sodi better, for he always enjoyed the inspiring and dramatic scenery of the earth. David, whose chariot has just gone, has very recently brought Seneca, mother and Mary with myself from the preparatory departments for children, which is far toward the southwest, to the children's amphitheater in the city where I have been for quite a time assisting the little ones in their first lessons in heaven. Seneca enjoyed the return trip through the mountain region splendidly, so I am sure you have chosen wisely."

"Now," said Gabriel, "when you are all ready we will be going, for we have to meet our Lord, with very many others, at the gate of Benjamin, which is toward the south-east. I wish for Seneca and Bohemond to sit with me."

We took our places beside the angel, while mother, Genevive and Mary sat together in the rear. In a moment more our chariot moved away.

"Oh, Seneca, you blessed of God," said the angel. "You are a chosen vessel, selected for a special errand by the Lord Himself."

"Oh, tell me, Gabriel, what is before me. Heaven has been one glad surprise at every turn since I stepped from the angel's chariot, at a distant portal of paradise when we first entered this kingdom of glory."

"Everything is before you," said the angel, "almost nothing behind in comparison to what is yet beyond. But Seneca, you are a favored saint of God and the unfoldings of His intentions toward you will be made known in due time."

At this, mother, who was intensely interested in the conversation, spoke and said, "Oh, Gabriel, the man by your side is my own son and was cared for by these hands from the day of his birth and I am deeply interested in all that is transpiring."

Genevive now stood to her feet in the chariot and leaning forward wrapped her arms around my neck and said, "Oh, Gabriel, this man was my husband on earth and most sweetly were our earthly lives spent together. But here we are joined in an eternal union."

At this the angel laughed and said, "Are you married again?"

"Oh, no, we are not married, for saints do not marry in heaven, nor do they wish to, but these bonds of highest friendship will be eternal, will they not?"

"Sure," said the angel. "Your love and oneness will be far sweeter than ever it was on earth."

"But I would like to know," said Genevive, "and I know you can tell me, if the angels themselves were ever in love among themselves with a love similar to that of husband and wife?"

At that question, Gabriel reduced the speed of his chariot and turned his head to glance over his shoulder at Genevive, who stood with her arms still about my neck. He said, "You have almost put me to blush for we are inferior to you, who have descendants and creations of your own. We have no bride neither bridegroom. But marriage was such a leading passion with the inhabitants of the earth that our Lord intends perpetuating it in eternity, only changed. He is now and ever will be the bridegroom and all the saints, you, not us, will be his bride. We were the working bees of the great family of man on earth and in heaven, neither drones nor queens, but we are all content with our sphere of action. We know no sorrow nor any un-fulfilled desire which cannot be fully met here in heaven or on earth. We are your servants, and this trip to the gate of Benjamin and to paradise is my joyful service."

At this Mary stood up and said, "Oh, Gabriel, this man by your side is my father, from whom I parted when only just an infant. I think it must have been your own chariot which brought me to the care of dear grandmother as I learned to call her later."

At this the chariot stood still and the angel arose and turning himself around, he laid his hands upon our heads with the blessings of the chief angel of God and said, "Oh, ye saints of the Most High, I was present when the morning stars sang together and tuned my harp to that sacred melody of the skies. I am the same now as I was then. But before you is an endless progression, an eternal destiny, with exaltations, honors, and blessings of which you know but little now.

"Now," continued Gabriel, "we must be going, for soon we must join others at Benjamin's gate."

The chariot moved on with great speed. The scenery was all new to Bohemond and myself, and Genevive said it was almost new to her. The mansions were beautiful with all the decorations that any soul in heaven could wish.

Thousands of saints were coming and going, like a hive of busy bees.

"I see David's chariot," said the angel, "coming down that broad avenue over there." In a little while we were side by side, with greetings and congratulations, for his chariot was now filled with ancient men and women—saints of renown.

On the chariots moved, side by side; we went till at last the shining of the wall began to appear and the great gate of Benjamin loomed up before us and as we were reducing our speed, we noticed the most beautiful chariot we had yet seen standing just near the gate. It glittered with the gold of heaven, set with diamonds of beauty. Our Lord Himself was in that chariot. His twelve apostles also were with Him. Such a halo of light, almost with dazzling brightness, shown all about that chariot. In a few moments the three chariots stood side by side. We all bowed our heads, saints and angels together, before Him who had prepared this city for us.

David's harp was of great proportions. He stood before us all and announced a hymn. We all arose and sang the praises of our Lord and Redeemer again while standing in the chariot.

gel Gabriel sang an ancient solo with loud hosannas.
o was in David's chariot, and who was a close friend of
said, "Sing it again," and surely the sweetest music to
had ever listened rolled from his hallowed lips.

"Now," said the angel, "look through this gateway," and
behold, there was an immense company of new arrivals standing
just outside, and singing some new songs. This company had
been escorted here from different places in paradise much
the same as we had been only a short time ago. Stephen, the
martyred saint, had led this company.

While he was getting them ready to pass through the gateway
into the presence of their Lord Jesus, who now invited us all to
a raised elevation close beside the gateway, He laid his hand
gently on my head and said, "Son, be of good cheer, your earthly
mission is not yet completed, but as I once called Moses and
Elijah from these shining gates, so now I send you to make
known what you have seen and heard, which is but a little of
what you shall yet see, but this is all they will receive at your
hand now. True unfeigned faith in many sections of the earth
is waning. You will find a faithful helper, on whose head my
blessings shall rest. When you have completed your journey to
the earth, I shall confer the elder's blessing upon you—an earlier
inheritance of the 'purchased possession.'" All heads were now
bowed, while He prayed and committed me to the angel's care.

Bohemond and the women came close to my side and said, "Is
it true we must part?"

"Only for a time, yes, only for a time." And with great cheer I
said loudly, "I shall soon see you again."

The Lord said, "Hurry to your mission. I must welcome
these outside the gate, for I have redeemed them by my blood."
So saying, He called Gabriel to His side and gave him a charge
concerning me.

I said good-bye to my kindred and all those who came to see
me off, saying, "I will see you again," and I climbed aboard the
angel's chariot.

*   *   *

Visit with Daniel

The angel now was seated by my side and his chariot moved slowly away. As I looked backward while we were passing through the great arch of the gateway, I saw many of them waving with their hands a good-bye blessing.

We were soon passing beside the great company who were eager to enter the gateway. We gave them all a bow of recognition, saying, "We will see you all again." We were soon beyond the hearing of their voices. As the chariot vanished from their view, we were rapidly flying along an immense roadway, leading them from the gate of Benjamin to distant places of paradise. Great fruitful valleys spread out everywhere, and thousands of busy saints were gathering the ripening fruits.

"Now," said Gabriel, "over there are the mountainous regions of paradise of which I spoke; shall we go past them?"

"Oh, angel, my cup of blessing seems full and will contain no more. The task that I have been charged with is consuming all my thoughts, but if you are willing, just a quick flight by the foothills will please me much and satisfy my curiosity."

He quickly turned his chariot to a side road leading up the mountain slopes. Rapidly we were climbing those stupendous heights. On a lovely plateau half way up the mountain summit, Gabriel brought his chariot to a stop just to allow me to look out over the vast plains and valleys of paradise. Immense gardens of beauty, filled with all varieties of fruits and blooming shrubbery were spread out as far as the eye could reach. I could see at a glance multiplied thousands of busy saints and angels enjoying these luxuries of heaven. My soul was so filled with the ecstatics of glory and praise for these exalted privileges which our good Father had granted me, and the honors conferred upon a mortal man of earth, that I was simply lost in wonder and fell down at the feet of the angel with adoring praise to God. "Oh, Gabriel, stop your hand of blessing, my cup runneth over."

"Now, Seneca, we must resume our journey." With great speed the chariot darted down the great hillsides and across the valleys, through lovely parks and pleasure grounds of paradise. Thousands of honored saints have their mansions in the various sections of this dramatic scenery of heaven. I was so overcome

with the grandeur of this section of paradise, that I fell down at
the feet of the angel again and poured forth my praise to God
with loud hosannas. I arose and the angel pointed toward a great
paradisical arch in the far distance. Toward it he was steering his
chariot. The trees of life were growing everywhere. The aroma
of the leaves made the breath of heaven fragrant with their life-
imparting virtue. No picture on earth could ever suggest such
glory as this.

The angel drove his chariot slowly amidst deep gorges and
past sparkling fountains and where groups of men and women
were going and coming, or refreshing themselves at the fountains
and with the fruit of the trees of life. I said to the angel again,
"What a place to spend the leisure hours of eternity, in rest and
recreation! Surely this is heaven!"

The angel now turned to me and asked if I recognized him.
"Oh, Gabriel, at the Throne I saw you."

He said, "Think again. When you left your earthly habitation
for this most favored tour of heaven."

"Oh, angel, you brought me to the gates of the Kingdom."

"Indeed," said the angel, "and I have another mission for you.
Only a glimpse of the heavenly inheritance and the greatness of
our Father's house have you yet seen, but eternity is yet before
you and it alone will suffice to satisfy your inquisitive soul. But
now a little quiet rest is needed before your next mission begins
and before we pass through that great archway over there."

Gabriel drove his chariot very slowly along. Hundreds of
new arrivals were to be seen with their first rapture of delight
in heaven. This I knew from their behavior, which was so much
like my own had been. Some just stepping from the chariots were
shouting just as we had done.

On the chariot went toward the great archway of paradise.

I leaned my head on the shoulder of the angel and for the first
time felt a kind of drowsiness come over me. I slept: how long,
I do not know, but when I awoke, the chariot was standing still
at the threshold of the old home at the foothills of the Cascades.
I stepped out and was met by two angels who led me inside. I
said, "Is it true that I am back again to my earthly home?" Sure
enough, for there lay my body which had been carefully guarded

by my faithful servants, Sena and Serva, who had previous
instructions for no burial for fifty days. More than forty had
already passed and yet upon the body though cold and in the
slumbers of death, no signs of decay were seen.

It was midnight and the watchers were sound asleep. Gabriel
now joined us and laying his hand upon the faces of those who
slept, there followed the deep sleep which came over Adam
while Eve was being formed from his rib. So no one of the
sleepers knew of our presence. Gabriel now passed his hand
over the lifeless body and instantly it sprang into life with a
mighty change from mortality to immortality. In a moment it was
my own again. I shouted, "Oh, glorious body! Oh, redemption
of the purchased possession! Mighty change—from death to
immortality!" Oh, how quickly I thought of the words of Paul:
"For our conversation is in heaven, from whence also we look
for the Saviour, the Lord Jesus Christ, who shall change our vile
body, that it may be fashioned like unto His glorious body."
(Philippians 3:20-21) I stood a moment in wonder, not knowing
what to say. I was so overcome with the glory of God, but body
and soul became as one.

I now said to the angel, "Who will assist in this work
committed to me?"

He quickly directed me to you, my son,[19] explaining the place
of your home. "But we will not leave you," they said, "until all
things are adjusted. Now leave your earthly home and all therein.
They will take care of themselves. Come to the chariot."

The Cascades and the Rockies were passed and the valley
of the Mississippi was soon behind us. Near your humble
village the chariot stopped. I have crossed the continent to find
you, my brother, and now I am so glad you have so willingly
and cheerfully assisted in this work. I have examined your
manuscript and approve of what you have done. Let the printer
take it from your hands. Put it before the people. Some will not
approve, others will bless God. But if you faithfully complete
your task, the blessing of Almighty God will be upon you.

---

19. Addressing Reverend Scott, the transcriber, that is.

The Story Ends...

Mr. Secenca Sodi then came and pressed a kiss upon my forehead and turning away, he said, "Farewell, my son. The blessings of the eternal God be yours, blessing you both in basket and in store. The eternal God shall be your refuge and underneath shall be the everlasting arms. (Deuteronomy 33:27) He shall convert thine enemy to your friend, and the angels which so faithfully guarded my mortal body, shall guard your soul." Again he pressed my hand in his, kissing it again and again, and lifting up his eyes and hands toward heaven, he pronounced the blessing of heaven upon me, and in closing said, "The angel is waiting for me," and he vanished out of my sight. I quickly followed to the door, but he was gone, for the chariot had borne him aloft.

The End

END NOTES

The original version we obtained contained these following interjections by the author, mainly regarding his interaction with Seneca Sodi as he transcribed his testimony.

Many of these digressions also broke up the testimony in chapters, which the current publishers feel is a distraction to the story as it draws too much attention to the act of transcription. The original chapter divisions have not been preserved but for a line of asterisks in the text, but all other original comments have been preserved as follows:

a.

"Now," said Seneca, "I must leave you for the night. You are weary and tired and must sleep. I will see you again on the second evening from this," and he vanished from my room. I sat musing. Where has he gone? Where does he stay? What is his food? Has he now no human association on earth? Can he not reveal himself to others as he has to me? When he comes again I must entertain him and find out, if possible, other secrets of his sojourn on earth.

* * *

The day with its busy cares was passed. The evening was lovely indeed. The stars had just begun to show their presence in the twilight and I was waiting in my library at the appointed hour. The door opened and Seneca Sodi came in. I arose to greet him, and said, "Good evening," and tried to clasp his hand in mine, but felt no touch of a material palm to mine as is usual. He replied: "I am glad to see you, my son. Are you prepared?"

I told him I was, but felt a strange feeling of awe mingled with fear. His spotless purity seemed to come before me, and my own sinfulness and unworthiness was so apparent, but I summoned all my courage and said, "I am ready for your message."

He asked me, "Have you faithfully transcribed the previous message?" I told him I had and showed him the manuscript. He quickly looked it over with satisfaction and said, "You may now write," and he proceeded as follows:

b.

"Now," said Seneca, "you are weary and need sleep. May God's good angel guard and give you rest." And so saying he vanished.

* * *

On the second evening again I was waiting for him, not knowing certainly, however, that he would come at that time. But I hardly had my studio in shape for such a visitor until he was by my side. His garments shone with a peculiar brightness and his face was all aglow with the light of heaven. I said, "Seneca Sodi, do take a seat and explain to me the mystery of your body and your food. Both your hand and the fruit of your basket evaded the grasp of my hand."

"At another time, my son, I will make it clear to you. Are you ready for my message?"

"I am," I replied. He then proceeded as follows:

c.

"Now," said Seneca, "I must let you rest, you have faithfully served me, and are weary. I will see you again on the second evening," and he bade me good-night and was gone.

* * *

At the appointed hour my silken bearded friend came in and with the usual greeting I welcomed him into my studio and said, "Seneca Sodi, I am most deeply interested in your narrative, and was eagerly waiting your coming."

"Are you ready?" he asked. I told him I was He then proceeded as follows:

d.

"But," said Seneca, "I cannot describe to you these wonders tonight, for you are already weary." So saying, he bade me goodnight and was gone.

* * *

The sun was just setting when Seneca came again. I was on my knees in prayer, and as I opened my eyes he was standing by my side. "I greet you again tonight, my son," he said, "and with God's blessing upon you, we will now proceed with the narrative." He commenced by saying:

e.

At this Seneca Sodi stood up and said, "My son, I will see you again at the appointed time. The blessings of God Almighty be upon you, and among these blessings cause His face to shine upon you and give you rest." I looked up from my writing only to see him vanishing from my room.

f.

"Now," said Seneca, "I must leave these holy men and the chariot till I see you again," and so saying he bade me goodnight.

* * *

I was very eager for Seneca's return for he had left the chariot filled with men en route for the children's Polytechnic and the remainder of his narrative I was exceedingly eager to hear.

A gentle rap at the door, it opened, and my silken bearded friend stepped in. "I am glad to see you, Mr. Sodi, I have always welcomed you, but never more than tonight. I have everything ready for your message."

"You shall write it, my son," he said, and he began:

g.

"Now," said Seneca, "I must leave you rest. The hour is late and you are tired."

"But," I replied to him, "are you not tired also?"

"No, I never tire any more, nor ever feel weary, but I long to get back to my Father's house. Just as soon as my task to the world is done through you, I shall speed with all haste to my treasures above. Be of good cheer, my son. A reward is in waiting for you." So saying he bade me good-night and vanished from my sight.

* * *

"You are on good time tonight, Seneca, and I am rested and ready for my evening's task."

"I am glad," said Mr. Sodi, "to see you in good humor and in such fine spirits. May the Almighty Father bless you tonight as I give you my message:

h.
(But of this matter I will speak to you again later, if you wish.)

i.
Seneca now said, "You have written enough for this night. Transcribe all carefully and I will see you again as usual," and so bade me good-night.

* * *

(I freely confess that by this time I was so carried away by the wonderful revelations of Seneca Sodi, that I could scarcely think of anything else, day or night, and after he would leave me some nights I would dream I was in heaven and walking the same streets where I had gone in vision and on waking felt disappointment that I was not there.)

But it was now time for his return. My manuscript and everything was ready. Really, I was eager for his coming, for I was eager indeed for another trip into paradise and further to see how saints in heaven assist each other. A rap was heard on the door and Seneca came in.

"Good evening," he said, and came and gripped my hand with that peculiar touch that only the hand of a spiritual body can impart.

I welcomed him to a seat, but he said, "Where is your manuscript?" He quickly looked it over, with a smile and nod of approval. "Only," he said, "I fear we have not put the soul and spirit of my concern into the message as we should have done. The eager concern I have that it may stamp itself upon all who read, that they may feel the importance of a due and rightful preparation for the life to come, for men do not know what they are doing when they trifle with the vast concerns of an eternal scene, but when you, dear son, have done your best, God will bless your effort and mine, for it has been sent."

After I again assured him I would do all I could to faithfully declare his message, he took his seat near me and began as follows:

We closed our last meeting while in David's chariot at the gateway of the children's great amphitheater and were planning a tour to a distant point in paradise.

j.

"Now," said Seneca, "you must rest for a few minutes, and while you rest will you share in the fruit of my basket?" I put out my hand to take what seemed a beautiful orange, but I could not grasp it. I seemed mortified to think he was eating and I could not.

"Why is it?" I said.

"This fruit," said he, "is but a tiny sample of what I have been telling you about. You will not forget that the heavenly world is a spiritual kingdom, and all things have a spiritual nature, and truly you can only eat of this fruit after you have crossed the boundary of your earthly habitation."

* * *

"You may now write again," said Seneca.

k.

"Now," said Seneca, as he turned to me, "you may rest for the night. Faithfully transcribe and make the message plain." He turned his back and with a pleasant good-night, disappeared from my room.

l.

At the appointed hour Seneca came in. He seemed to hasten to his usual place for his story left him sitting in the chariot at our last meeting.

"My son, have you everything ready for the message?"

"I have," I replied, and he proceeded as follows:

m.

Seneca Sodi now said, "I leave you, my son, for a little rest."

I threw myself back in my chair with my eyes closed and reverently thanked my God for such revelations of the unseen world.

"Oh, how real is the future life," I said. "I devoutly wish I was there now. No trouble, no sorrow, no death. Oh, heaven, not far away, may thy gates be opened for me, and may the angel's chariot hasten to my humble cot!" I thus mused and prayed until I was fast asleep.

* * *

Seneca Sodi returned and said, "You may write again," and he proceeded as follows:

n.

"Now," said Seneca, "you are weary and must rest. Sweet sleep and the peace of God be with you!" As I looked toward him, he vanished from my sight.

* * *

Seneca came as usual and glancing over the manuscript, he suggested a few changes here and there and then proceeded as follows:

o.

"You may now rest," said Seneca Sodi, "for I know you are weary and tired," and handing me the scroll to be copied with care, said good-night.

p.

* * *

The evening was most lovely indeed. Seneca Sodi came as usual, very full of pleasantness and joy, and glancing over the manuscript, especially the scroll, suggesting a few corrections here and there, he said, "Are you ready for me, my son?"

"Indeed, I am eagerly waiting for your message," and he began:

q.

"Now," said Seneca Sodi, "you must rest. Faithfully transcribe what I have given you and I will see you again soon."

As usual, he bade me a kindly good-night, and was about to vanish from me when I said, "Oh, Seneca, my soul is so ravished with your narrative that I wish you would remain all night and take me through the great congregation."

"You will hear me again, my son," he said and was gone.

* * *

Seneca came again as usual. His face was beaming with great joy and gladness.

I said, "Why are you so exceedingly happy tonight?"

He quickly replied, "Because I am going to take you tonight where I long to be myself."

"Well," I said, "I am eager for your message. When you left me last night, we were traveling very near the Throne."

"Yes, my son, and I will tell you more of it now."

r.

Seneca now said. "Faithfully transcribe and I will see you again as usual. Good-night."

* * *

I was eagerly waiting for Seneca's return, to know further, myself, the things of the Throne of God. He was on time and greeted me with his usual pleasant smile and said:

s.

"The revelations he gave us, I will not describe tonight. I must leave you now," said Seneca. "You are tired and have need of rest," and he vanished from my presence.

* * *

Seneca came bright and early His face was beaming with holy joy and light. He quickly looked over the manuscript and was pleased and said, "This part of your task is nearly done. Fully carry out all the further details and you will not be disappointed in your rewards."

"When I left you last we were eating some fruit nearby a fountain on the east side of the Throne and ...

About Edward Johnson and '40 Days in Heaven'

Edward Johnson originally found this manuscript on line at www.spiritlessons.com, made his own hand bound copy and was reading it one day when the Lord spoke to him, "You don't need to keep those chapter divisions."

First looking down at his homemade copy, he then looked up to the sky and asked, "Why? I've already printed my own copy." To which the Lord replied, "I want you to republish this story. Do it as a *first fruits offering* of your book publishing ministry."

That prophetic word started a long editorial process that eventually led to the 2008 printing of the first edition of *40 Days*. Despite many challenging obstacles, the "first fruit" 1,000 copies were done just before the Christmas holiday that year and distributed to the community in Hong Kong, some to the Philippines, USA and others mailed across the world, all for free, despite many personal financial struggles. But the fruit of this sacrifice was soon to manifest as stories immediately circulated back about lives that were touched, hearts healed, hope restored and faith renewed by this classic spiritual gem, seemingly lost for many years, now restored and edited for a wide, modern audience. A year later the book was prepared to be released for sale, and, under the watchful care of the Lord, is again spreading its wonderful message of hope and truth around the world in printed and audio form.

Edward is called and serves as a Prophet of the Lord, along with his wife, but they also serve the community in other ways, spending much of their time training and equipping the saints, especially in inner healing, *spiritual communion* with the Lord (which is learning to speak with God in two-way conversation through the indwelling Holy Spirit, something every believer can do regardless of gifts), and prophecy.

They also have their own book titles, such as *Foundations of the Kingdom*, a book containing revelation from the Lord about the shift out of the church age, into the Kingdom on earth, and other titles on prophecy and ministry. They also publish a monthly journal of prophecy, *the Hong Kong Intercessor*, which is available for free from the website www.kingedwardltd.com, which you may also enjoy.

KING EDWARD LTD

makers of the
Hong Kong Intercessor,
Journal of Prophecy and Intercession.

WWW.KINGEDWARDLTD.COM

Made in the USA
San Bernardino, CA
17 June 2015